"*Unleashing Peace* is packed \ teachings, readable truths, and a sense of well-being as I turnec ̣ ̣ ̣ ̣ ̣ ̣ ̣ ̣ ̣ ̣ ̣ ̣ ̣ book, drinking in its biblical message."

Robert J. Morgan, bestselling author and
Teaching Pastor at The Donelson Fellowship

"I have never known a time when the promise of peace seems more elusive. Anxiety and depression are at an all-time high, yet Christ promised us his peace. In this in-depth yet practical book, Jeremiah provides a road map to accessing the peace of God. This is more than surviving; we are offered the gift of truly flourishing."

Sheila Walsh, author of *Holding On When You Want to Let Go*

"With the incisive mind of a scholar and the tender heart of a pastor, my friend Jeremiah Johnston charts a course for how you can live out *shalom*—peace, happiness, joy—in your life while encouraging wellness in others. Here's a powerful biblical antidote to despair!"

Lee Strobel, *New York Times* bestselling author, Strobel Center
for Evangelism and Applied Apologetics at
Colorado Christian University

"As a mental health expert, I can tell you there's hope in these pages. As I have read each chapter, you, too, will discover the transformation of God's truth for you. Allow for a new peace to develop and grow as you walk through the carefully crafted hope plan in these pages. You will be blessed as I was!"

Gregory L. Jantz, PhD, bestselling author
of more than forty books

"I've spent a lot of time lately pondering how much Jesus cared about the human condition. Salvation isn't just our ticket to heaven; it's the promise of wholeness, restoration, well-being, peace, and redemption. In *Unleashing Peace*, my friend Dr. Jeremiah Johnston brilliantly explores our God-given invitation to know and walk in the wholeness of God."

Susie Larson, national speaker, talk radio host,
and author of *Fully Alive*

"If you desire more peace, more happiness, and more understanding of what the Bible has to say about these important topics, Dr. Johnston's new book will be transformative for you. It is one of the most significant Christian resources addressing mental health I've ever encountered."

Dave Willis, pastor, podcaster, and author of *Think Like Jesus*

"The potential of this book to transform faith communities, wider society, and the world as a whole is enormous. If readers embrace the deep theological insights it contains, they will not only experience the deep peace of God, but also be able to bring that peace to others."

Paul Foster, Professor of New Testament and Early Christianity,
School of Divinity, University of Edinburgh

"Peace is crucial yet elusive. Whether it is political, relational, or internal, we long for and try to grasp peace with all our might. Allow Jeremiah Johnston to take you on a journey, with both the mind of a scholar and the practicality of a missionary, to finding and sharing a deeper understanding of the shalom of God."

Gregg Matte, Pastor, Houston's First Baptist Church

"Few are better positioned to provide practical answers to the tsunami of painful life-issues facing our world. Dr. Jeremiah Johnston—apologist, theologian, and speaker—here unpacks the depth of true, biblical shalom. This book is a must-read, must-share opportunity to bring sustainable hope into lives today."

Rev. Dr. Luke Biggs, Peace Lutheran Church,
Grand Island, Nebraska

"The church needs this book. Jeremiah Johnston tackles the mental health issues the body of Christ often avoids. Shalom is powerful in deliverance. I found hope and encouragement in *Unleashing Peace*."

Dr. Ted H. Traylor, Pastor, Olive Baptist Church,
Pensacola, Florida

"Whenever I publicly reveal my own lifelong struggles with anxiety attacks and OCD, some well-meaning Christians react with dismay that I'm not being 'spiritual' enough with my solutions. Mental health has long been ignored in the church, leading to lives of confusion and despair for many believers. *Unleashing Peace* is a Christ-centered reset, a superb resource not only for personal growth but also for group study."

Rene Schlaepfer, Senior Pastor, Twin Lakes Church, California

"In a fallen world where people are triggered by brokenness and seemingly unshakable mental and emotional pain, *Unleashing Peace* brilliantly charts a course for triggering the peace and well-being of God—in your life and the lives of others. No matter where you are on the 'mental wellness trajectory,' as Jeremiah so thoughtfully puts it, there is something in this book for you."

Rick Renner, author, teacher, pastor, and
broadcaster, Moscow, Russia

"We see about ten thousand media messages and touch our phones about two thousand times a day. In the most distracted culture in the history of the world, our desperate cry is for 'happiness.' And yet the shallow answers found in self-help books and social media only make it worse. That's why *Unleashing Peace* is so important.

You'll discover what real happiness is and a new perspective on how to achieve real peace."

Phil Cooke, PhD, writer, media producer,
and author of *Maximize Your Influence*

"Peace is desperately needed in our generation and culture choked with mental health issues and the chaos left in the wake. God's peace is the answer to bring hope and healing to a hurting world. This book should be essential reading for every pastor, professor, and leader."

Jack Graham, Pastor, Prestonwood Baptist Church

"It is highly commendable when biblical scholars draw practical applications that potentially alleviate unrest for believers. Jeremiah Johnston does just that throughout this volume. Highly recommended."

Gary R. Habermas, Distinguished Professor, Liberty University

"There is so much brokenness in our world today. As a pastor I have the privilege to meet with and preach to people weekly who are deeply troubled, experiencing hardship and struggling through the issues of life. What is needed now more than ever is hope, and this is what Jeremiah Johnston offers—a message the church needs to hear, pastors need to communicate, and Christians need to share."

Jarrett Stephens, Senior Pastor, Champion Forest Baptist Church,
and author of *The Always God*

"Dr. Jeremiah Johnston speaks to an important yet neglected topic. *Unleashing Peace* is a much-needed book for today's world—a world that has little peace and little hope. I recommend it highly."

Craig A. Evans, John Bisagno Distinguished Professor of
Christian Origins, Houston Baptist University

"I cannot think of anyone who would not benefit from learning how to access the sunshine of God's shalom, forsaking the shadows of anxiety, depression, fear, shame, or unbelief. *Unleashing Peace* is a powerful tool to have in your arsenal."

H. Edwin Young, Senior Pastor,
Second Baptist Church, Houston

"Peace is God's blessing on his children, yet so many fail to find it in life. Jeremiah has unleashed a very practical book that delivers sound reasons for *why* each believer should dwell in peace, as well as practical ways *how* one finds that peace."

Mark Lanier, author and founder, Lanier Theological Library

"I struggled, intensely, for thirty-five years with the pain of mental disease in the form of OCD, even while pastoring a large church. My life is a testament to God's healing, but we also need the help of other gifted believers like Dr. Jeremiah Johnston."

Jeff Wells, Lead Pastor, WoodsEdge Community Church, Texas

"A radiant narrative of hope, *Unleashing Peace* is an immensely readable, biblical, and psychologically credible engagement with emotional health. It could be one of the most important books in our post-pandemic generation."

Rev. Will Van Der Hart, The Mind and Soul Foundation

"*Unleashing Peace* is your guide for discovering and living in God's gift of peace. As leader of Christian Thinkers Society, Jeremiah is committed to helping us know Christ and experience his grace. This book is alive with the hope and comfort we need in these chaotic days."

Philip Nation, speaker and author of *Habits for Our Holiness*

"Jesus is the Prince of Peace. Peace is one of the fruits of the Spirit. So why is there so little peace in the world, even among Christians? Jeremiah Johnston helps us recover and apply these forgotten truths."

Warren Cole Smith, President, MinistryWatch.com

"There are many qualities to this remarkable work by Jeremiah Johnston. It not only fits the times, it engages the Scriptures and the deepest questions of our hearts."

Robert Sloan, President, Houston Baptist University

"I'm honored to share words of endorsement for this amazing book. Dr. Jeremiah has been a huge blessing to Oasis Church every time he visits, and having the opportunity to read *Unleashing Peace*, I am confident that Oasis will once again be blessed by every word they read."

Ricardo Garcia, Executive Pastor, Oasis Church, Florida

"*Shalom* is such a pregnant word. All of the Bible is about God bringing shalom to chaos through Jesus. We live in a chaotic world, which is why I am excited to insist you read *Unleashing Peace*. Jeremiah writes with the pen of a scholar and the heart of a pastor."

Dr. Brian Haynes, Lead Pastor, Bay Area Church and Christian School, Texas

"Thoughtful guidance to the breadth and depth of God's peace that is accessible, encouraging, and helpful for readers struggling with the very real challenges of our day. It is a joy to recommend this fine book."

David S. Dockery, President, International Alliance for Christian Education, and Distinguished Professor of Theology, Southwestern Baptist Theological Seminary

"Peace is one of the most common themes in the Bible. And yet it seems that so few Christians experience it. If you want to know genuine peace in your life, this book is a biblically-based, practical guide."

Sean McDowell, PhD, Biola University professor, speaker, and author

"After two decades of pastoral ministry, I am learning more and more that the situations people go through do not 'steal' God's peace from their lives as much as they 'reveal' that they did not have God's peace to begin with. Jeremiah Johnston teaches readers how to rely on God's promises rather than human explanations and experiences. Prepare to find peace as you read this book."

Christian Newsome, Lead Pastor, Journey Church International

"There is no one unaffected by mental health struggles, either directly or indirectly, and Christians are hungry for answers to the big questions about depression, anxiety, and suicide. I've personally seen the phenomenal response from audiences when Jeremiah has spoken about these issues. Jeremiah's new book is also one of the most helpful responses I have encountered."

Justin Brierley, show host of *Unbelievable?* and author of *Unbelievable? Why After Ten Years of Talking with Atheists, I'm Still a Christian*

"In a world plagued by the sigma that comes with working through mental health challenges, *Unleashing Peace* offers a fresh yet timeless biblical perspective on a topic the church so often fails to address. This book will equip Christian leaders in helping others discover God's shalom."

Adam C. Wright, PhD, President, Dallas Baptist University

UNLEASHING
PEACE

UNLEASHING
PEACE

EXPERIENCING
GOD'S SHALOM
IN YOUR PURSUIT OF HAPPINESS

JEREMIAH J. JOHNSTON

BETHANYHOUSE
a division of Baker Publishing Group
Minneapolis, Minnesota

Published by Bethany House Publishers
11400 Hampshire Avenue South
Minneapolis, Minnesota 55438
www.bethanyhouse.com

Bethany House Publishers is a division of
Baker Publishing Group, Grand Rapids, Michigan

Library of Congress Cataloging-in-Publication Data is on file at the Library of Congress, Washington, DC.

ISBN 978-0-7642-3082-0 (trade paper); 978-0-7642-3971-7 (casebound)

The information in this book is intended solely as an educational resource, not a tool to be used for medical diagnosis or treatment. The information presented is in no way a substitute for consultation with a personal health care professional. Readers should consult their personal health care professional before adopting any of the suggestions in this book or drawing inferences from the text. The author and publisher specifically disclaim all responsibility for any liability, loss, or risk, personal or otherwise, which is incurred as a consequence, directly or indirectly, of the use of and/or application of any of the contents of this book.

Cover Design by LOOK Design Studio

Author is represented by Law Office of Curtis W. Wallace, P.C.

Baker Publishing Group publications use paper produced from sustainable forestry practices and post-consumer waste whenever possible.

21   22   23   24   25   26   27   7   6   5   4   3   2   1

For Lily Faith Johnston

Mental pain is less dramatic than physical pain, but it is more common and also more hard to bear. The frequent attempt to conceal mental pain increases the burden: it is easier to say "My tooth is aching" than to say "My heart is broken."

—C.S. Lewis, *The Problem of Pain*

CONTENTS

FOREWORD

Many people today have a flawed perspective of God. For some reason—whether it be bad experiences in their past, false teaching, or just misconceptions that our culture has reinforced—they would label God as authoritarian, distant, critical, angry, disconnected, judgmental, or vindictive. They see God as someone who is just waiting for them to screw up so that he can punish them.

How incredibly sad.

The true God—the God of the Bible—is a God who is happy and who wants us to be happy too. In fact, since we are made in his image, you could almost say we have been prewired for happiness. We are prewired for hope. We are prewired for peace.

Does that mean Christians should always go around with a phony smile plastered on their faces? Of course not. Christians experience deep loss, pain, and heartache, just like other people. But the happiness, hope, and peace that I'm referring to go deeper than just emotion. Feelings come and go, but the peace—the shalom—that you are going to read about in this book is a peace that passes understanding and stems from a relationship with the One who created us. He is the Author of happiness, hope, and peace. He is the Source of wholeness and well-being.

When our son Christopher went to be with the Lord suddenly in a car crash more than a decade ago, I remember feeling complete and utter devastation—like I could curl up and die at that moment. In the days that followed, I felt profound sorrow and emptiness. I wept often and I wondered why God would allow such a thing to happen. As time has passed, the loss has remained, but the emotions have changed, softened, transformed into another kind of grief and aching. There is still sadness, but it is a different form of sadness. It's something that my wife, Cathe, and I will never "get over." It will remain part of our lives until we see Christopher again in heaven.

But I can honestly tell you that through all of it, the shalom of God—the peace and presence that Jesus Christ offers—was, and is, real and steadfast. The promises of Scripture that I had preached for so many years withstood the test of true-life experience and came through the fire as gold.

God's peace is not dependent on circumstances. It is a deep and abiding assurance that God is true, that he is with us, and that he will make all things work together for good to those who love him and are called according to his purpose. The shalom of God is the assurance that he who started a good work in us will be faithful to complete it until the day of Jesus Christ.

We live in a world where people are desperate to experience the peace, the hope, and the happiness that only God can offer. They are broken, longing for healing and wholeness.

This is why I am so happy to commend to you this dynamic new book by my friend Jeremiah Johnston, *Unleashing Peace.* Jeremiah has the mind of a scholar but with a common touch to take the complex and make it understandable.

I pray that as you read this book, you will be equipped, energized, and inspired to share the gospel of peace with others.

Let the peace of Christ rule in your hearts, since as members of one body you were called to peace.—Colossians 3:15 NIV

—Greg Laurie
pastor and evangelist,
Harvest Ministries

The Most Important
Question of Our Time

It was spring when I found myself on a flight from Houston to speak at a gathering for hundreds of pastors in central London. The Holy Spirit had been prompting me to address the biblical response to mental illness and anxiety. That's when I saw a photo I will never forget.

If you have spent any time at all walking the busy streets of greater London, you learn quickly that pedestrians do not have the right-of-way. If you try to cross a street, watch out! The North Circular Road near Golders Green in North London is no exception. The busy intersection features a large footbridge so walkers can cross above the heaving traffic below.

A photo of that bridge, along with a news story, had appeared in my in-box. The report said that around 5 p.m. local time, with rushing cars below, a man had made it out onto the outside ledge of the bridge, threatening to jump.

In an act of incredible compassion, at least a half dozen strangers—men and women making their way home from work across the footbridge—quickly collapsed around the man. They would not let go of him. And that's the photo I saw, of the heroic passersby holding the man for two hours until a hydraulic lift eventually lowered him to safety.[1]

The photo captured a display of love and determination to rescue. One of the first things that stands out is a yellow rope lassoed around the man. God works in mysterious ways—yes, someone evidently had a rope that particular day. Another person has their arms clutched through the bridge bars around the man's calf muscles. Another individual is clasping the man's belt. Finally, another man is seen an inch from his face, looking the man in his eyes. He appears to be saying something, and his arms are around the man's neck and shoulders. Like the others, he will not let the man go.

For all we know, the strangers were not mental health experts. None of them knew each other before the incident. These good Samaritans saw a dire situation and immediately acted. A life was saved.

In my talk at the London event, I showed this photo, and the response was palpable. My message? God never gives up on anyone. We give up on people. God does not. We should never stop trying to save people from themselves.

It saddens me that the church is woefully behind in helping people with mental health issues, because every single person is somewhere on the mental wellness trajectory. Mental wellness is a conversation that includes all people of God. We should be the ones wrapping our arms around those with chronic worry, mood disorders, anxiety, anxiety attacks, posttraumatic stress disorder (PTSD), depression, and suicidal thoughts. And whether we struggle with mental illness ourselves, or know someone who does, it affects us all. According to the World Health Organization, depression is now the leading cause of disability in the world.[2]

This is a global issue. It is an individual issue. And I believe it is the most important question the church can answer today: How can I find true happiness and peace?

We founded our ministry, Christian Thinkers Society, for the sole purpose of inspiring believers to follow the Great Commandment of Jesus: to love God with all your heart, with all your soul, and with all your mind. The other side of our missional vision and objective is inspiring thinkers to become Christians. In other words, you don't need to check your brain at the door to become a follower of Jesus. Far too many Christians are soft targets for the ebbs and flows of skeptical, anti-God messaging. Christianity is not antithetical to education or thinking; in fact, the opposite is true. There is a persuasive body of truth that as the Christian faith has been passed along, people have thought deeply about it and it has become the foundation through which we address issues of the liberal arts, humanities, politics, philosophy, the arts, social sciences, natural sciences, media, journalism, and music—the whole spectrum. Why? Because all truth is God's truth.[3] Since all truth is, in fact, God's truth, we have a firm belief that any truth we find in the world can and will be reconciled with our faith.

Jesus' ministry to "seek and save the lost" was a restorative ministry. His restoration was certainly spiritual, but it did not stop there. The healing, forgiving, loving relationship Jesus won for us at the cross penetrates every aspect of our lives—spiritually, mentally, physically, and emotionally. These days, the popular term for that is wellness. The Global Wellness Institute defines *wellness* as the active pursuit of activities, choices, and lifestyles that lead to a state of holistic health.[4] As I see it, Jesus was talking about and teaching wellness before anyone, but he used a different word: *shalom*—the best form of wellness there is.

Back to our bridge photo for a moment. Where are you on the bridge? If you're the person who is on their way to the outer ledge, I want you to know, you can be saved. Or, maybe you aren't feeling that depth of despair, but you feel beaten down and troubled, and long for relief and happiness. God's Word has great and precious promises available for you right now. And if you consider yourself one of the individuals walking across that bridge, not needing help this moment but wanting to intervene and help someone who is struggling or even in crisis, this book has a message for you, too, with practical steps and the theological underpinnings to allow God to use you to unleash his peace and protective presence in the lives of those around you. No matter where you are on the bridge, there is a path to peace and joy and happiness.

In the pages that follow, I speak from my experience as a Bible scholar to clarify, teach, and expound on what the Bible actually says about how we think and specifically how we can renew our minds, which is a command given to us in Romans 12:1–2. I also clear up some "problem passages" from the Bible that are often misunderstood. Further, I highlight some frequently neglected passages that speak to God's peace in our lives. I write to teach you how to unleash the shalom of God! If we are called to be Christian thinkers, it naturally follows that the Bible has much to teach us about right thinking. As such, this book should also be a resource for Christian leaders, pastors, and educators, Bible teachers, and Christian counselors, therapists, and psychologists, but by no means is it a replacement for these vital disciplines. The fact remains, we need more Bible scholars and theologians to bring biblical precision to the trending questions of our culture. It is sad that we often spend time answering questions at the seminary and higher education level that no one is asking in the real world.

The real problem we face is that people see Christianity as an answer to yesterday's questions, and hence they think it offers no relevance today. What we need to do is translate our faith language into what C.S. Lewis calls the "cultural vernacular."[5] We need to actually think about how we translate our faith language into today's language but also answer the questions people are asking.

You should know that I never planned to write a book like this. But after I wrote a book called *Unanswered* to tackle people's top questions rarely addressed in church, I was thanked most for addressing suicide and mental health. As Christians, we need to build awareness of the problem and remove the stigma, because mental illness is widespread and affects everyone. A Lifeway Research survey found nearly 70 percent of pastors rarely or never address the subject of mental illness from their pulpits, and the same survey revealed that the majority of churchgoers wish their pastors would discuss it.[6] The satirical Christian website The *Babylon Bee* even highlighted the problem with a story headlined by "Nation's Churches Announce Plan to Continue Ignoring Mental Health Issues":

> In a rare moment of interdenominational unity, the nation's churches announced a plan to continue ignoring mental health issues among congregants. Despite increased awareness of mental health issues in the nation overall, hundreds of churches agreed not to do anything at all about the ongoing crisis in the country. "We vow to continue pretending mental health issues do not exist, and simply encouraging our members to pray the sadness away," a representative for the coalition said Wednesday. "This truly is the best way to solve a problem: by pretending it doesn't exist."[7]

For more than a decade, our ministry's presentations, conferences, media broadcasts, and other events have featured question-and-answer sessions. Partnering with churches across all denominations (and non-denominational), universities, and other apologetics and worldview ministries in the United States and internationally, has exposed me to the pressing questions from a wide context of the Christian faith.

It is clear we have missed the mark in passing on what I call a "theology of shalom" in our lives. God wants us to experience joy, and that's what we experience when we have a faith in God that is guided by the facts of Scripture.

The words *joy* and *rejoice* appear almost three hundred times in Scripture. Several times in his letter to the Christians of Philippi, Paul speaks of joy and urges the people to rejoice. The psalmist

For Ministry Leaders

Research shows that individuals experiencing psychological distress are more likely to seek help from clergy (a pastor, priest, or rabbi) before any other professional group, including mental health experts.[8] This reveals what you may already know: The church is central in the healing equation for the multitudes who are seeking peace and joy but struggling with anxiety. There is a great opportunity for Christian leaders and the global church to minister to the afflicted. That said, I have conducted scores of interviews with Christian leaders, and from my experience, many don't feel equipped to even know where to begin addressing the mental health crisis in our faith community. What's more, some don't feel capable or prepared to minister through this mental pain crisis because they themselves are barely coping and suffering in silence.

To show how relevant our faith is to the world around us, you need to be conversant in ministering in this space of mental wellness. If you lead Bible studies, teach Christian courses (at any level), coach young people, or practice ministry in any sphere, this book will equip you with the biblical tools to minister effectively.

says, "Take delight in the Lord, and he will give you the desires of your heart" (Psalm 37:4). And Jesus' famous sermon, the Sermon on the Mount (see Matthew 5–7), is a theological blueprint presupposing peace and happiness (or shalom) that is sorely lacking in so many Christian lives today.

"Nothing so educates us as a shock," wrote historian Will Durant.[9] The church has been shocked in recent times by suicides not only of Christians in the pews but of prominent pastors and leaders, as well. Suicide claims more lives than war, murder, and natural disasters combined.[10] And more years of life are lost to suicide than to any other single cause except heart disease and cancer.[11] I've noticed, though, that if we are not careful, we can develop a detached view of these grim statistics. Mother Teresa is known for saying, "If I look at the mass, I will never act. If I look at the one, I will." We must remember that behind all the statistics are very personal stories of "one," like the man on the bridge in North London.

In the words of Old Testament scholar Walter Brueggemann, "Shalom is not only an incredible gift, it is a most demanding mission."[12] How we come to not only understand the gift of shalom but live out shalom is central to following Jesus. This book charts a course for you.

In Part 1, you will learn the biblical principles for unleashing God's shalom into our lives. God wants us to be happy and at peace, constantly. *Happiness* is not a bad word for the follower of Jesus. Jesus describes a state of blessedness that could be interpreted as joy that includes laughing and giggling. Where did we get the idea that being a Christian means being a killjoy? The happy person is well—a healthier person. Proverbs 17:22 promises, "A merry heart does good, like medicine" (NKJV). This sense of delight and contentment extends vertically with God and horizontally with God's world around us. In Part 2, you will learn how to apply the wellness of shalom understanding by first understanding God's protective presence in our lives. God is our shield. Insofar as we understand God's protective presence, we will learn practically how to minister to those around us who are struggling in unwellness. In Part 3, you will learn about protecting the theology of shalom by answering some of the difficult passages in the Bible related to thinking and wellness, and maintaining shalom through the vicissitudes of life.

If you have felt alone in your pursuit of peace and happiness, I pray that through this book, you will feel seen and know that God cares about your pain and wants you to experience his shalom.

PART 1

UNLEASHING SHALOM IN YOUR LIFE

Wait, God Wants Me to Be Happy? *Really?*

I n one of the most heart-wrenching scenes in the Gospels, Luke records Jesus weeping over Jerusalem and saying, "If you, even you, had only known on this day what would bring you peace— but now it is hidden from your eyes" (Luke 19:41–42 NIV). We can sense the echo of Jesus' cry today as we appreciate the landscape of anxiety, despair, and depression around the world. *If you only knew what would bring you peace. . . .*

What a prayer, and what a profound statement.

We live in a time defined by some as hopelessness. Society is as fractured as ever. Virtual, social, and electronic connectivity has ushered in the unintended consequence of despair through the cancer of comparison. Stress kills people and poisons our bodies. Debilitating anxiety has become ubiquitous, unfortunately increasing in all age levels. Rates of major depression in teenagers increased 52 percent in the 2010s from the previous decade and 63 percent among young adults.[1]

While following the Prince of Peace, we seem to have lost our bearings for the path to peace. Indeed, in some fine Christian circles, an unintended consequence of critiquing the modern health-and-wealth gospel is that teachings have emerged that being happy as a Christian is somehow bad or even unspiritual to discuss. There are serious issues at stake, to be sure, but God is certainly happy, and he created us to reflect and glorify him. God's imparted shalom is the foundation, and experiencing happiness is one of the natural outcomes of following Christ!

After the name of Jesus itself, there is no finer word or concept than shalom (peace). *Shalom*, along with its variations, appears 550 times in the Scriptures.[2] Shalom originates from God himself and epitomizes the gospel and the active relationship God initiates, pursues, and perfects within each of us as his followers. Shalom is eschatological, for it looks forward through the eyes of faith to the resurrected and re-created cosmos, where everything and everyone will have shalom. Shalom is both active and holistic—active in the sense that shalom invites us to flourish.

One of the most overlooked aspects of balanced Christian living and teaching is the concept of unleashing the shalom of God into our lives. As we will learn in this chapter and the next, peace and happiness are not one and the same. But they are related. No one can be happy in a deep and meaningful way if they do not also possess peace. And those who possess God's peace are rarely unhappy.

Before looking at passages in the Bible that speak of happiness in the following chapter, let's review what the Bible says about peace—the state of being that is foundational to genuine human happiness. As we will learn, to receive the peace of Jesus is to be made whole and lack nothing.

Shalom: The Peace That Surpasses Understanding

Author and pastor Timothy Keller says *shalom* is one of the key words and images for salvation in the Bible. The experience, he says, is "multidimensional, complete well-being—physical, psychological, social and spiritual; it flows from all of one's relationships being put right—with God, with(in) oneself, and with others."[3] As I have mentioned, though, far too few Christians are familiar with shalom and its application in our daily walk.

The Hebrew word *shalōm*, which normally is translated "peace," occurs more than two hundred times in the Hebrew Bible, or what Christians call the Old Testament. Most of these occurrences in the Greek translation of the Old Testament (that is, the Septuagint) are translated with the word *eirēnē* "peace," from which we get the name Irene. In the Greek New Testament, *eirēnē* occurs some eighty-five times and means "to join" or "tie together into a whole," with a nuance of tranquility and harmony. Although the Greek word *eirēnē* is an acceptable translation of *shalom*, the two words are not identical in meaning and nuance. The basic meaning of the Greek *eirēnē* is peace in the sense of an absence of conflict or war. The Hebrew word *shalōm* can, of course, mean that, too, but it has a much deeper, richer meaning, as evidenced by one modern Bible version (NIV) that renders shalom seventy ways.

In the ministry and teaching of Jesus, we often find the word *peace* used in its Old Testament sense of completion and wholeness. Jesus taught us and exemplified that peace *with* God will result in the peace *of* God. For example, when Jesus commissions his apostles to go throughout Israel preaching the Good News of the kingdom of God, he instructs them in how to respond to those who variously reject or accept them and their message: "And if the house is worthy," Jesus says to the disciples, "let your peace come upon it; but if it is not worthy, let your peace return to you" (Matthew 10:13).

What does Jesus mean by "peace" in this context? Obviously, he does not mean the absence of conflict or the end of war. The idea that Jesus' peace can remain on a house (that is, on the people who live in the house—which in most cases means an extended family) implies something almost tangible about the shalom that Jesus offers.

Here's a key thought of application for us: Shalom implies that the blessing of peace with God, which includes forgiveness, assurance, and in some cases perhaps even physical health, will rest on the household that embraces the message of Jesus. However, should a household reject the Good News of the kingdom, this peace will not remain on that household. God's peace fulfills, restores, and makes complete.

We see this concept of a restoring peace in the New Testament story of the woman who suffered with the hemorrhage.

And there was a woman who had had a flow of blood for twelve years, and who had suffered much under many physicians, and had spent all that she had, and was no better but rather grew worse. She had heard the reports about Jesus, and came up behind him in the crowd and touched his garment. For she said, "If I touch even his garments, I shall be made well." And immediately the hemorrhage ceased; and she felt in her body that she was healed of her disease. And Jesus, perceiving in himself that power had gone forth from him, immediately turned about in the crowd, and said, "Who touched my garments?" And his disciples said to him, "You see the crowd pressing around you, and yet you say, 'Who touched me?'" And he looked around to see who had done it. But the woman, knowing what had been done to her, came in fear and trembling and fell down before him, and told him the whole truth. And he said to her, "Daughter, your faith has made you well; go in peace, and be healed of your disease."

Mark 5:25–34

It is intriguing that the evangelist comments that Jesus perceived "in himself that power had gone forth from him" (v. 30). We must wonder if this is similar to what was just said about peace coming upon and remaining on a household that embraced the Good News of the kingdom of God. A suffering woman reached out to

Jesus in faith, touched him, and was healed. But it simply wasn't a healing power that went from Jesus to the woman; it was more. Jesus said to the woman: "Daughter, your faith has made you well; go in peace, and be healed of your disease" (v. 34). Again, the RSV translates it as "your faith has made you well," but the Greek literally reads, "Your faith has saved you." What has happened to the woman goes beyond mere physical healing. Healing, of course, has happened, and accordingly Jesus tells her, "Be healed of your disease." But the woman has been saved in every sense. She has been made whole; nothing in her life—physically or spiritually—is lacking. She may now "go in peace." When Jesus says, "Go in peace," he is not saying, "Have a good day." The peace of which Jesus speaks is life changing. It restores and makes whole. The woman who has been healed now possesses for the rest of her life that restorative, fulfilling *shalōm* that Jesus offers.

We encounter this idea again in one of the most tender stories in the Gospels, the story of the sinful woman:

> One of the Pharisees asked him to eat with him, and he went into the Pharisee's house, and took his place at table. And behold, a woman of the city, who was a sinner, when she learned that he was at table in the Pharisee's house, brought an alabaster flask of ointment, and standing behind him at his feet, weeping, she began to wet his feet with her tears, and wiped them with the hair of her head, and kissed his feet, and anointed them with the ointment. Now when the Pharisee who had invited him saw it, he said to himself, "If this man were a prophet, he would have known who and what sort of woman this is who is touching him, for she is a sinner." And Jesus answering said to him, "Simon, I have something to say to you." And he answered, "What is it, Teacher?" "A certain creditor had two debtors; one owed five hundred denarii, and the other fifty. When they could not pay, he forgave them both. Now which of them will love him more?" Simon answered, "The one, I suppose, to whom he forgave more." And he said to him, "You have judged rightly." Then turning toward the woman he said to Simon,

"Do you see this woman? I entered your house, you gave me no water for my feet, but she has wet my feet with her tears and wiped them with her hair. You gave me no kiss, but from the time I came in she has not ceased to kiss my feet. You did not anoint my head with oil, but she has anointed my feet with ointment. Therefore I tell you, her sins, which are many, are forgiven, for she loved much; but he who is forgiven little, loves little." And he said to her, "Your sins are forgiven." Then those who were at table with him began to say among themselves, "Who is this, who even forgives sins?" And he said to the woman, "Your faith has saved you; go in peace."

Luke 7:36–50

The evangelist Luke does not provide us with a full context. We are not told how it was that Jesus was invited to the Pharisee's house. The fact that Simon did not show Jesus the usual courtesies (greeting with a kiss, washing feet) suggests that the man had not really wanted to host Jesus. Perhaps he did so because he felt obligated to invite Jesus to dinner; otherwise, he would not have invited Jesus. So why did he? It could be that Jesus, as was his custom (Luke 4:16), had preached in the town's synagogue, and Simon, perhaps a ruler of the synagogue, was expected to provide Jesus with a meal. This would explain, too, how it was the sinful woman could be present. We should imagine a reception, open to those who attend the synagogue, taking place at the Pharisee's house—not indoors (the woman would never have been permitted entry into the house itself), but outside in a courtyard open to the public. In this setting, people would be free to come and go, including a woman of ill repute. However we are to understand the setting, what unfolds at this meal was not what Simon expected.

When Simon observes the woman ministering to Jesus, he assumes that Jesus is no prophet. After all, a true prophet, as a holy man, would never permit a sinful woman to touch him, not even his feet. Moreover, a true prophet would possess the power of clairvoyance (as did Elisha, for example) and so would know "who and what sort of woman this is who is touching him" (v. 39). Had Jesus possessed such power and therefore had known who the woman truly was, he would not have allowed her to touch him. At least that was what Simon thought. But not for long.

Jesus turns the tables on Simon, for Jesus knows what Simon is thinking! That Jesus knows Simon's thoughts is seen in the brief parable that Jesus offers. *Who will have the greater love for the generous, forgiving creditor?* Simon rightly answers, "The one, I suppose, to whom he forgave more" (v. 43). Jesus then looks at the woman—the very woman Simon had been thinking about—and says that he knows of her "sins, which are many" (v. 47), but her extravagant expression of love for Jesus demonstrates that these many sins "are forgiven." The story ends with Jesus assuring the woman, "Your faith has saved you; go in peace" (v. 50).

In this story, there is no physical healing, but there is spiritual healing. The woman's sins are forgiven, she is "saved," and she now may "go in peace." The peace that Jesus has given her is the same that he gave the woman who had suffered from the hemorrhage, and it is the same that will be offered to households who receive the Good News of the kingdom of God. It is a peace that heals, restores, and makes complete. Again, to receive the peace of Jesus is to be made whole, to lack nothing.

When Jesus approached the city of Jerusalem a week or so before that fateful Passover, crowds greet him shouting, "Blessed is the King who comes in the name of the Lord! Peace in heaven and glory in the highest!" (Luke 19:38). The peace that the crowds anticipate is not absence from war, but the restorative peace that God in heaven has promised to make available to his people when the Messiah comes. The tragedy, however, is that this much desired peace will not come upon Jerusalem. As surely as the peace of God will not rest upon the house that rejects the Good News of the kingdom, so the peace of God will not rest upon Jerusalem, for the city's rulers will reject Jesus and, at the hands of Roman authority, will have him executed.

This is why Jesus, as he approaches Jerusalem and looks upon the city from the vantage of the Mount of Olives, weeps and says, "Would that even today you knew the things that make for peace! But now they are hid from your eyes" (Luke 19:42). What are these "things that make for peace"? They are two: repentance and faith. If Jerusalem responds to the message of the kingdom the way the sinful woman did at Simon's house, then the peace of God will come upon the city. The city and her inhabitants will be restored and be made complete. Alas, it was not to be. The city rejected Jesus, sent him to the cross, and forty years later was surrounded by the Roman army and destroyed. Foreseeing this dreadful fate, Jesus weeps for the city (and days later will explicitly prophesy the coming tragedy).

There is no doubt that this sorrowful prophecy troubled the disciples of Jesus. They entertained hopes of salvation, of a new government, of the enthronement of their master. Under the leadership of Jesus, the Lord's anointed—Jerusalem and all Israel—would experience a revival and a restoration never before seen. Or so they hoped. But it was not to be so. Rather, the salvation of Israel and of the world itself would be achieved paradoxically on a Roman cross at Calvary. It is not surprising at all that the disciples found this difficult to accept. Jesus addressed this fear and confusion in his well-known "farewell discourse" in the Gospel of John (John 14–16).

In this discourse, Jesus speaks of peace in two passages. In the first, he says, "Peace I leave with you; my peace I give to you; not as the world gives do I give to you. Let not your hearts be troubled, neither let them be afraid" (John 14:27). The explicit contrast between the peace Jesus gives and the peace the world gives is very intriguing. What did Jesus mean? By "world" Jesus means either the Jewish leadership, which opposes Jesus, or he means Caesar and the Roman Empire. Indeed, Jesus may have meant both. The "peace" of the Jewish leadership, centered in the high priest and his ruling priestly colleagues, was one of collaboration with the

Roman authorities. This meant oppression of most of the Jewish people in Israel. Even worse, the ruling priesthood was itself corrupt. We know this not only from Christian sources, like the Gospels and Acts, but from non-Christian Jewish sources themselves. Josephus, the Jewish apologist and historian who survived the great rebellion of 66 to 70 AD, says in his writings that the Jewish ruling priests were corrupt, oppressive, and hated by the common people. Indeed, when the Jewish rebels gained control of Jerusalem, they murdered the high priest and then looted and burned his house. In later writings, Jewish rabbis say the same thing: the ruling priests of the first century were corrupt and violent.

But the "world" that Jesus in John 14 principally had in mind was the Roman world, of which first-century Israel was a part. One of the Roman imperial slogans was "peace and security." Paul alludes to this slogan in his first letter to the Christians in Thessalonica: "When people say, 'There is peace and security,' then sudden destruction will come upon them as travail comes upon a woman with child, and there will be no escape" (1 Thessalonians 5:3).

Epictetus, the late-first to early-second-century Greco-Roman philosopher, alludes to this political propaganda when he assures his readers: "Caesar has obtained for us a profound peace. There are neither wars nor battles, nor great robberies nor piracies, but we may travel at all hours, and sail from east to west" (*Discourses* 3.13.9, LCL). One oft-cited inscription in Halicarnassus, Asia Minor, from the time of Emperor Augustus (ruled 31 BC–14 AD) declares:

> Land and sea have peace [*eirēneuosi*], the cities flourish under a good legal system, in harmony and with an abundance of good, there is an abundance of all good things, people are filled with happy hopes for the future and with delight at the present.[4]

This is Roman imperial propaganda at its best. How many people really saw the world this way at this time is hard to say. A major part of the justification of Caesar's supreme authority was his guarantee of "peace and security." But only God, through his unique Son, Jesus, can offer genuine peace and security; and the peace that God offers is not simply absence of war, but a healing, restorative wholeness. Jesus offers his disciples *his* peace ("my peace I give to you"). This is not the phony, unsatisfying peace of Caesar; it is the saving, fulfilling peace that comes from a Savior who suffers and dies for his people. Therefore, the followers of Jesus should not worry. As Jesus exhorts his disciples, "Let not your hearts be troubled, neither let them be afraid" (John 14:27).

In the second passage in the farewell discourse in the Gospel of John, Jesus returns to this theme. He tells his disciples, "I have said this to you, that in me you may have peace. In the world you have tribulation; but be of good cheer, I have overcome the world" (John 16:33). We again hear the explicit contrast between the peace Jesus offers and the peace that the world may promise but cannot offer. "In me," Jesus says, "you have peace." But "in the world you have tribulation." The disciples will face tribulation in the world for two reasons. One reason is that the world simply cannot provide anyone with genuine, restorative, fulfilling peace. No one will find completion and wholeness in the world, apart from God and his redemptive work through Jesus. Another reason the disciples will have tribulation in the world is that the world will turn against them, even as it will turn against Jesus himself. Jesus assures his disciples that he has "overcome," or "conquered," the world. Jesus has again subverted the Roman political propaganda that claims that it is Caesar, regarded by many as a "son of god," who conquers the world. Not so, it is Jesus, the real Son of God who has achieved a lasting, genuine victory.

Perhaps no one among the first-century followers of Jesus understood God's *shalōm* better than the apostle Paul. Before he met the risen Jesus on the road to Damascus (Acts 9), Paul (or Saul, as he was also known) was not a peaceful man. He fiercely persecuted the Jesus movement, even to the point of death. After his conversion, he admitted that he had tried desperately to justify himself by following the law of Moses in a strict manner. But when he met Jesus, he began to understand what peace really was.

Several times in his letter to the Christians of Rome, Paul mentions peace. For example, because believers are "justified by faith" in Messiah Jesus, Paul says, "we have peace with God" (Romans 5:1). Pastor Timothy Keller helps us understand again the weight of this passage and concept as it relates to Paul's statement in Romans 5:1: "This peace cannot increase or decrease."[5] It was this peace that had eluded Paul in his earlier years. A statement like this would have stunned the pagans of the Roman Empire. In the pagan world, the gods were feared, even despised. They offered humans no peace, no assurance of salvation. In short, the gods had no love for humanity; they cared not a whit. But meeting the risen Jesus changed everything for Paul. In Jesus he found peace. He found joy. And he found life.

Perhaps this peace has eluded you, as it did Saul of Tarsus? Have you placed your faith in Jesus, the King of Peace? The prophet Zechariah prophesied about the coming Messiah: "He shall speak peace to the nations; His dominion shall be from sea to sea, and from the River to the ends of the earth . . . I will set your prisoners free from the waterless pit" (Zechariah 9:10–11 NKJV).

Paul goes on to tell the Roman Christians that "to set the mind on the flesh is death, but to set the mind on the Spirit is life and peace" (8:6). Here "peace" can only mean that sense of wholeness and completion that the Hebrew word *shalōm* (from the verb *shalēm*, "to be complete, sound") often conveys. The mind that is set on the Spirit of God results in "life and peace." The one goes with the other.

Later in Romans, Paul defines the kingdom of God as "not food and drink but righteousness and peace and joy in the Holy Spirit" (14:17). Near the end of his letter, Paul prays, "May the God of hope fill you with all joy and peace" (15:13). Often, Paul describes

God as the "God of peace" (Romans 15:33; 16:20; 1 Corinthians 14:33; 2 Corinthians 13:11; Philippians 4:9; 1 Thessalonians 5:23). Peace is also a key part of the fruit of the Spirit (Galatians 5:22).

I can't emphasize it enough: Where God is, there is peace. Do you know the God of peace? Frequent contemplation of these Scriptures and others related to God's peace helps heal our minds and eliminates anxiety.

The most profound statement that Paul makes about peace is found in his letter to the Christians of Philippi. Imprisoned and facing an uncertain future, Paul writes near the end of his letter: "The peace of God, which passes all understanding, will keep your hearts and your minds in Christ Jesus" (Philippians 4:7). Paul did not learn this from someone. It wasn't something he was taught; he experienced it himself. After years of striving to find righteousness and striving for assurance that he was keeping the law of Moses perfectly and to know that he was saved, Paul met Jesus. For the first time in his troubled life, he was enveloped by the peace of God—a peace so transforming and so overwhelming it simply surpassed his ability to understand it.

The peace of God results in a state of genuine, meaningful happiness. Having met and embraced the risen Christ, Paul knows that he is forgiven and so can affirm the words of the psalmist: "Happy are those whose iniquities are forgiven, and whose sins are covered; happy is the man against whom the Lord will not reckon his sin" (Romans 4:7–8 paraphrased; cf. Psalm 32:1–2). Having experienced the peace, the shalom of God, Paul has discovered what true happiness is. And to the elusive concept of happiness we now turn.

How to Unleash Shalom and Happiness in Your Life

hen we're struggling with anxiety, depression, or doubt, it's easy to believe the toxic lie that we are a "second-rate" Christian whom God cannot use. The story of J.B. "Jack" Phillips shows how God uses us in our trials to encourage others in their trials. Phillips was one of the most influential Christians of the twentieth century. The author of over twenty books, including the classic *Your God Is Too Small*, he was also greatly supported and encouraged by C.S. Lewis. Phillips experienced two triumphs of grace in his life that should give all of us hope. God used him to translate the Scriptures and impact countless people through other writings, all while persevering through debilitating bouts of depression.

As a young man, Phillips arrived at Emmanuel College in Cambridge as an avowed atheist, wondering why God allowed his mother to die while in his teens. Indeed, he said, "The problem of human suffering is, I believe, the biggest serious obstacle to faith in a God of love today."[1] Yet, through the Cambridge Inter-Collegiate Christian Union (CICCU), Phillips became a Christian and sensed a calling to ministry. He eventually became a curate in a London church. During World War II, over twenty thousand Londoners were killed and a million homes destroyed during the Blitz. Phillips would sometimes preside over forty or fifty funeral services in a single week.[2] Still, he kept meeting regularly with his youth group, known as the King's Own. To encourage them, he would read Scripture to end each meeting. However, Phillips was disturbed by the dazed looks on the faces of his youth trying to understand the authorized version Scriptures. As wonderful as the King James Version is, if the youth were unable to grasp the truth of Christian hope with the Shakespearean language, what was the point? Phillips shared, "All my old passion for making truth comprehensible, and all my desire to do a bit of real translation, urged me to put some relevant New Testament truths into language which these young people could understand."[3]

So there Phillips was, huddled with his youth ministry and congregants in the bomb shelters of London, hearing the screaming bomb sirens, when he began translating the book of Colossians. Little did he know it would become his life's work. God met Phillips in the bomb shelters those days, and Phillips put his Cambridge classics education to good use and worked feverishly on what would eventually be called *The New Testament in Modern English*.

Unable to find a publisher for his new translation, Phillips took a step of faith and sent a copy of his version of Colossians to C.S. Lewis, whom he had long respected. It was August 3, 1943, when Lewis, at Magdalen College, Oxford, wrote back to Phillips and expressed his elation over the translation: "Thank you a hundred times. I thought I knew Colossians pretty well, but your paraphrase made it far more significant—it was like seeing a familiar picture after it's been cleaned."[4] At Lewis's urging, Phillips undertook translating all of the Epistles. Moreover, Lewis suggested a title for the work, *Letters to Young Churches*, and also asked his publisher, Geoffrey Bles (the company that published *The Chronicles of Narnia*), to take a serious look at Phillips's new translation. Little did any of them know, sales of *Letters to Young Churches* would total more than four million copies as Phillips's striking translation helped Christians rediscover the vitality of the Scriptures. Phillips's father, who was extremely hard on him, once told him, "You'll never earn your living by writing, my boy."[5]

By 1958, all twenty-seven books of the New Testament had been translated, and the full scope of his work was released as *The New Testament in Modern English*. Phillips's pioneering work cut a path for the unique modern translations that we all love and cherish today, including the English Standard Version, New King James Version, and the New International Version. According to Phillips's grandson, Peter Croft:

> He [Phillips] once said he sometimes got the impression that while he was working on the text, the text was actually working on *him*. Explaining this on a BBC radio broadcast on one occasion, he said, "I got the feeling that the whole thing was alive even while one was translating. Even though one did a dozen versions of a particular passage, it was still living." He said his translation work was like trying to rewire a house with the main electricity still on.[6]

As I mentioned, though, Phillips's work as a gifted author and communicator is only half the story, for he also struggled deeply with debilitating stress, anxiety, and what is now known as clinical depression. In his correspondence, he wrote that the people who are "most used of God frequently pay a very high price for it in personal suffering"—yet strength comes from the fact that even when Jesus faced the agonies of the temptation and the Garden of Gethsemane, he was not rescued from the situation but was "given strength to go through with it."[7] Phillips was blessed with a pastor's heart, shown in many ways, including this exhortation: "I beg you not to be unmindful of the unseen and often inexpressible sufferings of others."[8] And he often pastored people around the world through a vast written correspondence, as recorded to one who was having a difficult time: "As far as you can, and God knows how difficult this is, try to relax in and upon Him. As far as my experience goes, to get even a breath of God's peace in the midst of pain is infinitely worth having."[9]

As you might imagine, it was not popular in the 1960s for Christian leaders to discuss mental pain or depression. (Depression was not defined or understood then as it is today.) Eventually, Phillips would temporarily and voluntarily become a patient of a psychiatric clinic not far from his home. "I can only testify to the fact that it would have been of inestimable comfort and encouragement to me in some of my darkest hours if I could have come across even one book written by someone who had experienced and survived the hellish torments of mind which can be produced." Phillips went so far as to write a paper for psychiatrists tracing the main categories of his depression resulting from "self-condemnation" and the "agony of comparison."[10]

How did Phillips, known in many circles throughout the United Kingdom as the successor to C.S. Lewis, endure his depression and learn the peace of God? We see from his life that he sought counsel from trusted medical professionals. His loving wife also ministered to him through years of these occasional bouts. He did not allow his feelings to obscure the facts of his faith. And he was vulnerable about his struggles (we will learn more about vulnerability in chapter 6).

Through it all, Phillips said, "We can rest on the eternal and unchanging God. We may have to learn to trust this living God without any comforting feeling whatever, and this is no easy lesson to learn." Yet, Phillips proclaimed his depression was turned for good, because by it, he was "learning a deeper trust in the real and living God."[11]

For Phillips, as it is for us, the peace of God—which includes happiness and joy—is a discipline we learn, no matter what we face, not an automatic skill or natural Christian ability. Phillips's translation of Romans 12:12 is worthy of revisiting time and again:

> Base your happiness on your hope in Christ. When trials come endure them patiently, steadfastly maintain the habit of prayer.
>
> Romans 12:12 Phillips

Jesus Spoke about Happiness and Peace Together Frequently

Did Jesus use the word *happy*? Yes, many times. Was Jesus a happy person? I should think so! Jesus called his disciples and followers to a next-level type of happiness. Let us not forget, Jesus frequently made use of the Bible in his day (we have the living Word using the written Word!). *Happy* is a term Jesus picks up directly from the Old Testament.

In Hebrew, the word *blessed*, or happy, is *ashēr*; in Greek it is *makarios*. The first appearance of *ashēr* in the Hebrew Scriptures is in reference to the birth of Asher, one of the sons of Jacob the patriarch. When Leah, Jacob's wife, gives birth, she says: "'Happy am I! For the women will call me happy'; so she called his name Asher" (Genesis 30:13). Literally, Leah says, "With happiness I am happy, for women will call me happy." That Leah was overjoyed with happiness at the birth of her first son is hard to miss. It is not surprising that she named her son Asher, because the Hebrew word *ashēr* means "happy." (And, yes, even today Jewish men are named Asher, and Greek men are named Makarios.)

47

Almost all the other occurrences of *ashēr* in the Hebrew Scriptures—some two dozen—are examples of beatitudes (blessings). The first of these beatitudes comes from Moses, shortly before his death: "Happy are you, O Israel! Who is like you, a people saved by the LORD, the shield of your help, and the sword of your triumph!" (Deuteronomy 33:29). Centuries later the Queen of Sheba pronounces beatitudes on King Solomon (1 Kings 10:8; 2 Chronicles 9:7). Job, the righteous sufferer, pronounces a beatitude on the person whom God loves enough to discipline (Job 5:17). Most of the beatitudes appear in the Psalms. The psalmist sings: "O taste and see that the LORD is good! Happy is the man who takes refuge in him!" (Psalm 34:8). In another psalm we read: "Happy is he whose help is the God of Jacob, whose hope is in the LORD his God" (Psalm 146:5).

The best-known beatitudes are found at the beginning of the Sermon on the Mount (Matthew 5–7). Each one begins with the word *markarioi*, a plural adjective that can be translated "blessed" or "happy" (and because they begin *makarioi*, they are sometimes called makarisms). Our ears are used to hearing the word *blessed*, but I think it is better to use the word *happy*, because "happy" gets across the right idea in today's English. By the way, J.B. Phillips translated each of the beatitudes with the word *happy*! The beatitudes are as follows:

"Happy are the poor in spirit, for theirs is the kingdom of heaven.
"Happy are those who mourn, for they shall be comforted.
"Happy are the meek, for they shall inherit the earth.
"Happy are those who hunger and thirst for righteousness, for they shall be satisfied.
"Happy are the merciful, for they shall obtain mercy.
"Happy are the pure in heart, for they shall see God.
"Happy are the peacemakers, for they shall be called sons of God.

> "Happy are those who are persecuted for righteousness'
> sake, for theirs is the kingdom of heaven.
> "Happy are you when men revile you and persecute you
> and utter all kinds of evil against you falsely on my
> account."

Matthew 5:3–11 (modified to replace "blessed" with "happy")

The beatitudes of Jesus are surprising because of their paradoxical quality. Most people hearing this list will wonder in what way such people could be happy. In verse 3, Jesus pronounces a blessing on the "poor in spirit." In Luke's version it is simply "you poor" (6:20), probably meaning those who are economically poor. But Matthew's "in spirit" hardly softens the paradox, especially in the thinking of the Roman world. To be described as "poor in spirit" hardly conjures up the image of a proud, successful person. So, whether humble or poor (or both), such a person, Jesus says, is blessed or happy. The same could be said for the "meek," for they are hardly the kind of people who inherit anything, never mind the earth. Yet, they will.

Even stranger is Jesus' assurance that "those who are persecuted for righteousness' sake" are happy. Not many would think they are happy when they are persecuted—and not just persecuted, but persecuted "for the sake of righteousness." That is, Jesus says people are happy for doing the right and just thing, even if they are persecuted (and, perhaps, prosecuted, too, even imprisoned) for doing it. (In this connection, one thinks of the oft-heard, cynical comment that "no good deed goes unpunished.")

Those who have been given the peace, the shalom, that Jesus gives, are truly happy, even in the face of hardship, persecution, and tribulation. The remainder of the Sermon on the Mount underscores this theme. The happy are enjoined to "rejoice and be glad," for they stand in the company of the prophets and can look forward to a great heavenly reward (Matthew 5:12). The happy "are the salt of the earth" (5:13). They are "the light of the world" (5:14). They are those who heed the teaching of Jesus

49

and so possess a righteousness that "exceeds that of" the religious teachers of their time (5:20). They know the true meaning of the Law of Moses and so surpass the phony, self-serving application of the law often seen in the scribes and Pharisees.

The Truly Happy Take Jesus' Teaching Seriously

Happiness is not a feeling; it is a lifestyle, according to Jesus. The happy hear and understand the teaching of Jesus and know that he does not want phony religion but sincere piety and righteousness (Matthew 6:1–18). The happy among the followers of Jesus will lay up treasure in heaven (6:19–21) and will seek the kingdom of heaven (6:33). They will not judge others (7:1–5), but they will ask, seek, and knock, knowing that God will provide and open the door (7:7–11). The happy will "enter by the narrow gate," not by the wide gate that so many of the world try to enter—a gate that leads to sorrow and destruction (7:13–14).

Jesus pronounces beatitudes or "happinesses" elsewhere in his ministry. After describing his ministry to John's disciples, Jesus says, "Happy is he who takes no offense at me" (Matthew 11:6), that is, those who do not stumble over Jesus' startling and unexpected message of deliverance. Jesus has come not to destroy Israel's enemies but to save and redeem all, Israel and the Gentile nations alike. The mighty deeds of Jesus speak for themselves, and his disciples are most fortunate to witness them. So Jesus says, "Happy are your eyes, for they see, and your ears, for they hear" (Matthew 13:16). When a woman in the crowd cries out, pronouncing a blessing on the womb that bore Jesus, he replies, "Happy rather are those who hear the word of God and keep it!" (Luke 11:28, modified). The woman was not wrong, but happiness rests on people who hear the Word of God and take it to heart.

When Peter confesses that Jesus is the Messiah, the Son of God, Jesus replies, "Happy are you, Simon Bar-Jona! For flesh and blood has not revealed this to you, but my Father who is in heaven" (Matthew 16:17). The recognition of who Jesus really is has bestowed a happiness on Peter that he has never experienced. In a parable admonishing his disciples to be ready and alert, doing what they are supposed to be doing, Jesus says, "Happy is that servant whom his master when he comes will find so doing" (Matthew 24:46).

From these examples, we see that happiness can be experienced in various settings and for various reasons. This happiness is not laughter, it is not amusement, and it has nothing to do with something that is funny. It is a happiness that wells up within one's heart as a result of coming into contact with God and experiencing his restorative, life-changing shalom.

This is why the gospel, the Good News of the kingdom, is linked to peace. Isaiah the prophet made this connection centuries before Jesus began his ministry. The ancient prophet announced, "How beautiful upon the mountains are the feet of him who brings [the gospel], who publishes peace, who brings good [news] of good, who publishes salvation, who says to Zion, 'Your God reigns'" (Isaiah 52:7, modified). This passage, along with the similar passages in Isaiah (40:9 and 61:1–2), became foundational for Jesus and his apostles.

Isaiah's gospel of peace is heard in the words of the apostle Peter, who explains to Cornelius, the Roman centurion, "You know the word which he sent to Israel, preaching good news of peace by Jesus Christ" (Acts 10:36). The words "good news of peace" allude to Isaiah 52:7. Paul also quotes the passage, linking it to the promise that those who call on the name of the Lord will be saved (Romans 10:8–15).

Learning the Discipline of Peace and Happiness

Many wise pastors today are joining the chorus for the importance of biblical counselors, Christian psychologists, psychiatrists, life coaches, pastoral care, and helpful Christian friends. There's no question, these relationships are one of the keys to healing depression. Notwithstanding, as my friend Dr. Robert J. Morgan writes in *Worry Less, Live More*, there is no doctor like Dr. Jesus.

> We need a house call from the Great Physician and a good dose of His therapeutic truth. The Bible is our Lord's prescription pad, and meditation helps more than medication . . . the frequent contemplation of Scripture heals the mind. . . . We have to attack anxiety on the basis of spiritual truth, and I believe that's exactly how Paul dealt with his own issues of worry and stress.[12]

Now comes a hugely important point: As followers of Jesus, we have to *learn* peace and happiness. Mental, physical, emotional, and spiritual health is a never-ending battle. And the peace of God is unleashed when we are disciplined thinkers. Learn from everyone and every situation, but don't ever allow anyone else to think for you. Own your faith. Think through your faith. Live your faith as a discipline.

Peace and happiness come when our lives are anchored to God's unchanging truth. Unfortunately, too many Christians go to Google instead of God's Word when an anxiety attack hits.

Christian Thinkers Unleash Peace through Thinking

Peace happens through an action verb: thinking. But thinking about what, exactly?

Dr. Morgan calls Philippians 4:4–9 the greatest anti-anxiety verses in the whole Bible, "for they constitute the Bible's premier passage on the subject of anxiety."[13] I won't discuss the entire passage here, but note verse 9, where the promise of God's peace is preceded by *learning*:

> What you have learned and received and heard and seen in me, do; and the God of peace will be with you.
>
> Philippians 4:9

A few verses later (v. 11, 12), Paul states, "I have learned . . . I have learned."

Peace and happiness happen through learning in the Christian life, but how and what do we learn? What should we think about? Paul provides an answer in Philippians 4:8 (NRSV):

> Whatever is true, whatever is honorable, whatever is just, whatever is pure, whatever is lovely, whatever is commendable, if there is any excellence, if there is anything worthy of praise, *think* about these things.

The verb "think" dominates this verse and asks us to take into account all that is ours in Christ!

Timothy Keller said, "There's stupid peace and there's smart peace. The Christian's peace is not by making yourself stupid; it's by making yourself as aware of your beliefs, as thoughtful as possible."[14] We have to think about and focus on the ramifications of our beliefs. This is how peace happens. This is how happiness happens God's way.

Each time you experience anxiety, try to identify the lies you are thinking and instead focus on the truth. Common lies include: God has forgotten me. God doesn't love me. God has given up on me. I just committed that sin for the hundredth time. I am never going to make it. I am alone. I am a failure.

Absolute biblical truths include: There is a God who loves me. I am made in his image. My value is unchanging in his eyes. God is not a cosmic accountant waiting to smash me; rather, he is perfect in love toward me. God is reconciling and rescuing the world to himself through the sacrificial life, death, and resurrection of his Son, our Savior, Jesus Christ. Jesus will never, never, never, never, never, never leave me or forsake me. God is faithful. God is good. God is loving. God is merciful. God has a dynamic plan for everyone who loves him, so much so that he even causes all things (not just some) to work together for good in our lives.

God promises me wisdom for any decision I face. God promises me forgiveness in Christ for any mistake I've made. I don't live by my feelings; I live by faith in the facts of God's unchanging Word and character. Think about what is true about God, your position "in Christ," and ponder what Paul wrote: "We are more than conquerors through him who loved us" (Romans 8:37).

The content of our thinking determines our peace and happiness factor. Ask yourself: Am I trusting what I know is true in my life through Christ, or am I focusing on the problem, or adversity, to the extent that God is factored out of my situation?

Christian Peace and Happiness Is Unleashed through Gratitude

Another path to unleashing God's shalom in your life is walking in a state of gratitude. For one thing, gratitude has been found to block toxic emotions. Experiencing gratitude can also strengthen your immune system and even lower your blood pressure.[15]

The most popular class in the history of Yale University is "The Science of Well-Being," created by psychology professor Laurie Santos. Thousands of students have taken the "happiness" course in person and even more online. I watched some of Professor Santos's lectures, and one area that I really appreciated was her recommendation to keep a gratitude journal.

Make a list of all the good things in your life and read through them often. My friend Dr. Gregory Jantz, who started The Center—A Place for Hope, writes, "What has gratitude got to do with spirituality? Everything, because gratitude is a form of prayer. We are thankful *to someone*. Thirteenth-century German mystic Meister Eckhart summed it up: 'If the only prayer you ever say in your entire life is thank you, it will be enough.'"[16]

According to the science of well-being, one of the strongest indicators of personal mental health is our ability to experience and cultivate a life of gratitude. In Christian circles, we call this "counting our blessings."

The apostle Paul, led by the Holy Spirit, was on to something when he said we should not be anxious, but rather pray and live "with thanksgiving" and "the peace of God, which surpasses all understanding, will guard your hearts and your minds in Christ Jesus" (Philippians 4:6–7 NRSV). As followers of Jesus, our lives should be defined by gratitude. In fact, Paul, who has been called the apostle of gratitude, said the first step toward apostasy is ingratitude (see Romans 1:21 KJV; "neither were [they] thankful"). No wonder Paul said, "Rejoice in the Lord always; again I will say, Rejoice" (Philippians 4:4).

Gratitude confirms we did not accomplish anything on our own. Gratitude reveals a humble and dependent heart. In a corresponding letter, Paul connects the inner tranquility of Christ's peace with gratitude: "Let the peace of Christ rule in your hearts, remembering that as members of the same body you are called to live in harmony, and never forget to be thankful for what God has done for you" (Colossians 3:15 PHILLIPS). The basis of our peace and happiness and gratitude is the facts of our redemption and God's unfolding plan in our lives. The strength of our peace and happiness in Christ is based on God's promises.

Christian Thinkers Experience Peace by Applying Bible Promises

God's peace is based on his character and faithfulness to us. God's Word is unbreakable. It cannot fail because God cannot fail. Did you know there are 7,487 promises in the Scriptures from God to us? Do you know some of them? Are you applying these promises to your situation? When the anxiety and uncertainty attack our peace, do you have a promise to cling to? Certainly, many of God's promises are conditional, but what an arsenal of peace available to us.

For some, the Bible is like confetti. For me, it is a missile. The promises are targeted at the lies of the world, the flesh, and the devil. The promises are targeted at anxiety, worry, and problems. We have to memorize and meditate on God's promises to us if we are to live in a place of peace and happiness and unleash his reality (the God of peace) into our lives.

Here's a great promise to memorize and internalize: "And the peace of God, which transcends all understanding, will guard your hearts and your minds in Christ Jesus" (Philippians 4:7 NIV). Paul makes use of a vivid military metaphor to describe how the peace of God will allow us to relax and rest; imagine soldiers surrounding a city to protect it from invasion.

Paul says God's peace will keep guard over our hearts and our minds. Ralph Martin's commentary on Philippians reminds us of the word-picture from John Bunyan's classic, *Pilgrim's Progress*:

> Bunyan's use of this picture in the appointment and patrol of Mr God's-Peace in the town of Mansoul should be read in conjunction with this verse. "Nothing was to be found but harmony, happiness, joy and health" so long as Mr. God's-Peace maintained his office. But when Prince Emmanuel was grieved away from the town, he laid down his commission and departed also. It is a salutary reminder that we enjoy God's gift only *in Christ Jesus*, i.e., by our obedience to him and submission to his authority.[17]

Remember, too, from J.B. Phillips and other great heroes of our faith, that God will use us even while we struggle and strive for more of his peace. When we submit our lives to Jesus Christ and his Lordship, peace will be the result, but it is something we must contend for moment by moment in our faith. We are to constantly remind ourselves of all God has done, is doing, and will do for us. Finally, this is not to be interpreted as an individual peace alone. Let us never forget that Paul is writing these epistles to church communities. They were to worship in peace and unity, which leads to the next and most practical step to unleashing God's shalom and happiness in our lives: the ministry of presence.

4

The Ministry of Presence

For nearly half a century, an angel in human skin walked among sightseers of the sandstone cliffs known as the Gap, east of Australia's beautiful Sydney Harbor. In 1946, Don and Moya Ritchie settled in across the road from the Gap, where they lived until Mr. Ritchie's death in 2012, taking in the views of the glistening Tasman Sea. The sheer cliffs offered Australia's most picturesque views, but they also attracted desperate men and women pondering suicide. The Gap was so well-known that Alfred Hitchcock, international director and master of suspense, took time to visit the spot while premiering *Psycho* in 1960. He was photographed climbing the three-foot fence, pretending like he was going to jump.

For Mr. Ritchie, it was a place where he took people-watching to a new level. Living just fifty meters (164 feet) from the edge of the Gap, he would regularly approach individuals who seemed to be lingering a little too long overlooking the steep depression and ask, "Can I help you in some way?" He had a keen sense to spot would-be suicides and became known as the Angel of the Gap.

Officials credited Don with preventing 160 deaths, but according to his family, the number saved was actually between 400 and 500.[1] He would invite the hurting individual contemplating suicide to his home for tea or breakfast. As a younger man, Don even physically restrained the more determined from dying by their own initiative. One person later returned with a beautifully painted canvas featuring rays of sunshine with a profound epitaph: "An angel who walks amongst us."[2] Don would tell friends of those whom he saved, "I used to sell kitchen scales and bacon cutters, then I was state manager of a life insurance company. At the Gap, I'm trying to sell people life."[3]

Though Don never sought the limelight (especially so as not to attract others to the Gap with suicidal ideation), he was eventually recognized for his heroism in 2006 and awarded the Medal of the Order of Australia, the nation's highest recognition for outstanding achievement and service. Later, at a similar ceremony, Don used the occasion to highlight the importance of the small things one can do to save a life: "I ask each of you to consider how we can better support those contemplating suicide. . . . To my fellow Australians, never be afraid to speak to those who you feel are in need. Always remember the power of the simple smile, a helping hand, a listening ear and a kind word."[4]

Don was an exemplary member of the Greatest Generation. He served honorably as a decorated navy man in World War II, and he was stationed in Tokyo Bay when the Japanese signed the surrender on September 2, 1945. He went on to marry Moya and became a corporate businessman, father to three girls, and grandfather of five. Yet, he had no professional training or university courses in mental health crisis intervention. One Australian mental health expert clearly stated, "Don has saved lives because he has gone up to people and chatted with them."[5] And he did this for fifty years.

Don's life story illustrates the power of practicing what I call the ministry of presence, especially in moments of crisis. We do not need to have any "professional" mental health training to be a hero in another's life. This point cannot be overstated and is one we'll return to.

The "Presence Principle" Is Biblical

What does success look like in "religious life"? What does it mean to be a "good" Christian? What does it look like to truly follow Jesus? There are more than a few answers depending on who you ask. And you're not alone if you've wondered all this.

This was a trending question in the first century, too. So, let's allow the Bible to answer, shall we? And who is better equipped to answer the question than the Lord Jesus' brother, James.

By the way, recall that James did not believe Jesus was the Messiah before the resurrection, "For even his brothers did not believe in him" (John 7:5). It's not hard to understand James's predicament. What would it take for you to believe your older sibling was the Son of God and Messiah of the world? (When I ask audiences this question, people always laugh!) It was the same for James. Remember, the Bible tells us about real people, real places, and real events: amazing feats of faith, flaws, and everything in between. Likely, James was humiliated by Jesus' execution, crucified as an enemy of the state under the reign of Roman Emperor Tiberius (14–37 CE).

Paul, however, records a dynamic list of resurrection appearances by Jesus, including a specific appearance to his little brother that must have changed James's mind (1 Corinthians 15:3–8), for we are told elsewhere that James, along with Peter and John, becomes one of the "pillars" of the new faith (Galatians 2:9). This is why I look to James to answer our question about what following Jesus should look like in our daily lives, so here it is: helping people in their greatest point of need.

The Lord's brother, James, wrote: "Religion that is pure and undefiled before God" is visiting one "in their affliction" (James 1:27). The Greek word James originally used for our translated

English "affliction" is *thlipsei,* which is understood as one feeling pressure (literally pressed-in) in an oppressive state of physical, mental, social, or economic adversity. And I love the force of the Greek term James used for "visitation" because it illustrates our point: "to inspect with concern" (*episkeptomai*).

Key application: You are never more like Jesus than when you—with great concern (not condemnation or anger or frustration)—intervene with someone in their time of affliction. Your faith is never more real (pure) than when you inconvenience your schedule to help someone who is barely hanging on. The presence principle is how we must interpret and apply James 1:27 as we strive to meet people at their point of need and affliction (and we'll return to the rest of James 1:27 in a moment).

There were plenty of Pharisees in Jesus' day, and there certainly are in ours, too. We are not called to condemn, but to love with our presence. Perhaps you, like me, can remember specific moments in your life when a believer showed up in your life at just the right moment. They spoke a word of encouragement. They believed in you when others stopped. They forgave. They loved when you certainly did not deserve it. But they did so in Jesus' name. In effect, the short letter of James is a practical commentary of brother Jesus' Sermon on the Mount (Matthew 5–7). What does it look like to apply Jesus' powerful sermon to our lives? A significant indicator is our desire to help those who are hurting in the power and presence of Jesus' name! His presence is another aspect of the "Presence Principle." Perhaps you are thinking, *Okay, yes, I am on board, but how do I do it?* Well, you do not do it alone. Jesus leads you and loves through you with his very presence.

Jesus Embodied the Presence Principle throughout His Life and Work

A friend of mine has struggled with faith in God because a young, poor child died in his arms during his military service in a foreign country. In a moment of transparency and humility, my friend asked, "Where was God when she died?" To which another dear friend responded, "God's love and presence was there through you as she lay in your arms." Indeed, one of the key characteristics of Jesus' earthly ministry is both understood and interpreted through the lens of presence: that is, showing up when someone least expected it and at the point of greatest need.

Jesus' presence was felt in the temple, even as a boy, after he went missing from his family for three days. (By the way, can you imagine missing a child for three days? I am quite sure his parents were not very pleased.) Scripture says, "All who heard him were amazed at his understanding and his answers" (Luke 2:47). In John 3, Jesus' presence is powerfully attested in a visit from one Nicodemus at night. Luke recounts the impactful encounter of Jesus entering Jericho and, of all people, staying in the home of despised Zacchaeus, a tax collector and all-around scam artist. Yet, Zacchaeus felt seen, known, loved, and wanted in the very presence of Jesus (Luke 19:1–10). The Samaritan woman in John 4 is so moved by encountering the presence of Jesus that she exclaims to the whole city, "Come, see a man who told me all that I ever did" (John 4:29). Acts records the powerful encounter of Saul of Tarsus with the resurrected Lord Jesus (Acts 9:3–8; 22:6–11; 26:13–19). Walking into the presence of King Jesus utterly transformed Saul/Paul. Even the birth of Jesus is defined in terms of "presence."

This important theme of presence or being present; that is, *parousia*, which is the transliteration of the Greek παρουσία meaning "being present," is a key concept throughout the New Testament. The Latin equivalent of "Advent" or "Adventist" is certainly a term most followers of Jesus would find familiar. Due to our historical distance, we forget that this term in its original understanding had nothing to do with Christmastime or the incarnation of Jesus or even the Second Coming. In point of fact, *parousia* was understood contextually and originally in non-Christian literature as a life-changing encounter with the presence of the Roman emperor. The term is loaded with theological and political underpinnings, not the least of which is due to the fact that the emperor was worshiped as a god, or at a minimum, it was understood the gods accompanied the emperor with his presence (i.e., *parousia*). But the New Testament writers loved this word, understood it, and adopted it as God's all-powerful, saving presence through the resurrected Messiah, Jesus Christ.

One of the greatest promises of Jesus for believers is the fact that we are not only "in Christ" (see Ephesians 1–3), but Jesus also lives in us: "I in you" (John 14:20). When we live the "presence principle," Jesus manifests his powerful presence through our lives to others! We never do it alone. Unfortunately, in most churches today, "visitation" means following up on visitors and trying to persuade them to attend our church or become members. True biblical visitation is to tend to people who are in need, to be a presence, *the* presence of Jesus to them. We cannot overlook the importance. It's a ministry each of us are called to and for. Yet make no mistake, it is not easy. A godless world has no time for the outcasts, marginalized, and "inconveniences" of other people.

The world praises success at all costs. The cost of your family. The cost of your marriage. The cost of relationships. The cost of ethics. The cost of doing what is right in the name of doing what you can accomplish. Jesus' clear words from Matthew 25 turn our attention to the fact that the ministry of presence is all about not missing the opportunities in the mundane moments of life.

The Ministry of Presence Shines in the Simple Moments of Life

It has been said that busyness is the greatest enemy of good thinking. It is also an enemy of mental health. In addition to busyness, distractions define our times. Just look at how "on-demand" is now advertised on platforms from education to entertainment (and even ministry life at some levels), and how we are encouraged to "binge" this or that.

What is lost in all of this is the stillness of listening to God, taking spiritual inventory of our lives, and looking for opportunities to be the presence of Jesus for others. It's not impossible, though. I have personally heard powerful stories from successful and busy parents who were able to be present in their children's lives when they were encountering a crisis. One successful businessman said he never went home during the workday but felt prompted by God's Spirit to do so. He encountered his son in a crisis and saved his life.

Jesus' own words reflect the tension of being in his presence in the midst of distracted, busy living. Jesus discussed the power of his presence throughout the Gospel of Matthew. As we learned in the preceding section, Jesus manifests his presence through us and in us. Indeed, our experiences are Jesus' experiences: "He who receives you receives me" (Matthew 10:40). Let's also not forget the often-quoted promise of Jesus: "For where two or three are gathered in my name, there am I in the midst of them" (Matthew 18:20). But the key passage for understanding the presence principle is Matthew 25:31–46. Starting with verse 35 here, it reads:

> "For I was hungry and you gave me food, I was thirsty and you gave me drink, I was a stranger and you welcomed me, I was naked and you clothed me, I was sick and you visited me, I was in prison and you came to me." . . . "And when did we see thee sick or in prison and visit thee?" And the King will answer them, "Truly, I say to you, as you did it to one of the least of these my brethren, you did it to me."

Jesus' parable explores the reality that the most basic needs of human existence were met by others: food, drink, shelter, clothing, medical help, and care during imprisonment. Here, Jesus shows that in meeting the simplest, even basic needs of life, he will, in fact, meet every need in life; however, Jesus uses people. He does not FedEx blessings from heaven to your doorstep. God works always through human agency.

There are some important points of application from this passage. First, notice the surprise of the righteous doer practicing his presence. In the NKJV, verse 37 reads: "Lord, when did we see You hungry and feed *You,* or thirsty and give *You* drink?" When we remember all Christ has done for us in offering us forgiveness and an eternal inheritance (that is, unearned) with him for eternity, we will seek opportunities to minister to others who are downcast, as a reflection of God's work through us! The apostle Paul reflected these words in 1 Corinthians 12, discussing the church as a body of Christ in family: "If one part suffers, all the parts suffer with it" (v. 26 NLT).

Second, we learn from Jesus' words that we may be the hero in another's life and not even know it (until we come face-to-face with Jesus). Don Ritchie experienced this. Pastors are also well aware of this reality. When we help others, we don't need to bother keeping a record of it. The individual you intervene with may not even say "thank you" in the moment. Don't forget, ten lepers were healed by Jesus and only one bothered to return with gratitude (see Luke 17:11–19). And make no mistake, Jesus will remember and even reward every effort made in his name. The impact of ministering in Jesus' name is the fact that his presence will linger.

Third, Jesus emphasizing helping the "least of these" is the same as helping Jesus himself: "You did it to me" (Matthew 25:40). What a powerful picture painted by Jesus.

A special word of appreciation. A quick call of concern. A short but powerful prayer for another. Jesus commends the ministry of presence in the smallest (least) forms that make eternal impact on others.

In our busy world, we want to schedule everything around a specific calendar. To be sure, organizing and attempting to balance our lives is important. However, I have noticed the most life-changing encounters occur in the organic, unscheduled moments of life. God enjoys surprising us with his presence.

So how can we implement the "Presence Principle"? Two words: create margin. We have to resist the busyness of the time that pulls us from the unscheduled moments to be the presence of Jesus for others (and in so doing, experience His power in fresh ways in our own lives). And we have to fight to create stillness in our lives as an act of worship in which the Holy Spirit prompts us and leads us.

It was the Holy Spirit who prompted a good man in the New Testament to help, perhaps the most despised person in early Christianity.

The Presence Principle Trusts and Celebrates God's Work in People

In Acts 11 we meet Barnabas, a "good man, full of the Holy Spirit and of faith" (v. 24). Barnabas exemplifies the ministry of presence by never giving up on those whom God doesn't give up on. God is eternal and unchanging. He knows the whole story, and he doesn't give up on anyone. We, on the other hand, give up on people. It is a natural aspect of our fallen nature to judge and condemn instead of loving and helping others. Yet, when we are full of the Holy Spirit and faith, we become like God and celebrate his work in others, which always transcends human expectation.

In spite of the havoc that Saul of Tarsus wreaked on the early Christian movement, "Barnabas went to Tarsus to look for Saul, and when he had found him, he brought him to Antioch" (v. 25–26). Let's be contextually honest. Saul was public enemy number one for the early Christian movement. I don't think people could step back fast enough in volunteering to disciple, or even nurture, Saul's supposed newfound faith in Jesus. Yet Barnabas trusted God's work in Saul's life and even took the initiative to "look for Saul" in his hometown.

I need to ask: Whom are you looking for? Whom are the people who society, even the church, may have given up on or forgotten?

Barnabas also reached out to his cousin John Mark, to the point of breaking his ministry relationship with Paul (Acts 15:37–39).[6] John Mark deserted Paul and Barnabas on their first missionary journey, but Barnabas desired to forgive John Mark and give him another chance. Paul and Barnabas even parted ways over John Mark. It is interesting that much later, Paul refers to John Mark as a "fellow worker" (Philemon 24). And John Mark would also write the first canonical gospel: the book of Mark. Barnabas's life teaches us the presence principle will always trust and celebrate the work of God in others. Yes, our support of someone may involve accountability, but it should also be marked by compassion.

I have a few friends who believed in God's work in my life from the very beginning, before platforms, followings, logos, tours, books, and media. They are true friends. Be a true friend by trusting God's work in others.

The Presence Principle Requires No Official Prerequisites

Back to Don Ritchie for a moment. It is noteworthy that after fifty years of practicing the principle of presence for others at the Gap, most if not all of Don's award recognitions occurred in his eighties. One of the ugliest lies of Satan is that one is "too old" to be used by God (similar to the lie that you are too young for God to use you!). Indeed, it was in Don's later years that his story spread and had a far-reaching impact around the world. Still, his focus remained on the individual in crisis. "My ambition has always been to just get them away from the edge, to buy them time, to give them the opportunity to reflect and give them the chance to realize that things might look better the next morning."[7] Don was present, and he sought opportunities to show up at the perfect moment. Don shows us anyone can make a difference.

Unfortunately, too many people ignore loved ones or family members who are clearly in mental anguish. They do not know what to say, so they say and do nothing. This is a huge mistake. Compassionate conversations about suicide will not cause it to occur, but it can prevent it from happening. Failing to talk about suicide may have disastrous consequences.[8] You may not be an expert, but your care and compassion are essential. Your presence is mandatory. Please do something. This book discusses intervention steps and coping methods that are crucial. But first, you must decide to practice the presence principle. This is the most important step.

Kay Warren (an author and speaker), Steve Marshall (the attorney general of the state of Alabama), and I were speaking in Alabama at a conference about mental health called "Not Alone." This was the first public event for Steve since his wife had died by her own hand. Steve powerfully shared about his enduring faith and his wife's faith in Christ. I met with Steve and his daughter backstage, and she shared how she felt called to help others in crisis and desired to pursue a counseling degree. After my morning session at the conference, I will never forget a gentleman approaching me in tears and saying, "Today I learned we cannot just quote a Bible verse at someone who is in trouble. We have to be present in their lives." The Bible is powerful, to be sure, but truth is most powerful and effective when it is experienced in the context of relationship.

One final point must be settled in our minds, and I invite you to please share it with others. Did you know that when someone is experiencing mental and emotional trauma, non-experts are just as important as experts in the healing equation?

At another gathering, this one in Nashville, I spoke to about five thousand Christian counselors about the ministry of presence and how every person must step up and make a difference if the church is going to be present in the mental health crisis facing our world. Another presenter, Dr. Siang-Yang Tan, a professor of psychology at Fuller Theological Seminary, approached me afterward and shared some tremendous research he and a colleague, Dr. Eric Scalise, had done. They reported, "The majority of outcome studies comparing the effectiveness of professional therapists to lay counselors have found that lay counselors are generally as effective as professional therapists for most common problems."[9] The importance of this point is not that professional therapists are ineffective or unimportant, but rather, everyday people need to know they can help when friends and family face problems.

I have met hundreds of hurting parents, grandparents, and friends who regret they did nothing when a loved one was paralyzed in the quicksand of a crisis. Learn from the example of Don Ritchie. Ask God to help you to practice the principle of presence today. I pray the Holy Spirit has been speaking to you even while you have read this chapter. Whom is he speaking to you about? Now is the perfect time to pick up the phone, to meet that person for coffee, to practice the ministry of presence. You don't need prepared remarks. Don Ritchie asked a simple question with a smile: "Can I help you in some way?"

Jesus Is Our Shalom

William Thackeray's nineteenth-century novel *Vanity Fair* has been recognized as one of the best English language novels of all time.[1] Thackeray was so influential that Charlotte Brontë dedicated her novel *Jane Eyre* to him. Thackery described his book's setting "as a very vain, wicked foolish place full of all sorts of humbug, falseness and pretension . . . not a moral place certainly, nor a merry one, although very noisy—a world where everyone is striving for what is not worth having."[2] It is sad to say that his description mirrors the human soul today, with so many striving for what is not worth having.

You may not be aware that John Bunyan originally coined the term "Vanity Fair" more than 150 years earlier in *The Pilgrim's Progress*, describing a town called Vanity with a never-ending fair of evil organized by Beelzebub, Apollyon, and Legion. Christian and Faithful search for truth in Vanity and only find contempt. Faithful is burned at the stake, and Christian barely escapes with his life.

Then I saw in my dream, that when they were got out of the wilderness, they presently saw a town before them, and the name of that town is Vanity; and at the town there is a fair kept, called Vanity Fair: it is kept all the year long; it beareth the name of Vanity Fair, because the town where it is kept is lighter than vanity; and also because all that is there sold, or that cometh thither, is vanity.[3]

Like Christian and Faithful, perhaps you have found yourself looking through the stalls of your own Vanity Fair. There is no truth for sale in Vanity Fair, though, only lies—lies that lead to anxiety, distrust, despair, and loneliness.

The Scriptures tell us "there is no peace . . . for the wicked" (Isaiah 48:22) and again, "there is no peace for the wicked, says my God" (Isaiah 57:21). If we have learned anything in this book, it is this: Anything that costs you your peace is too expensive. But how do we *find* peace? How do we *recognize* peace? How do we *know* peace? Truth is the first step. For Jesus said, "I am the way, and the truth, and the life; no one comes to the Father, but by me" (John 14:6).

Peace to You!

It is Sunday night, April 5, AD 33, and gathered together behind locked doors is the faithful group of disciples along with, we can speculate, the women mentioned in Luke 8 and 24. The day has been *full* of empty-tomb discoveries and resurrection appearances. Early Sunday morning, Mary Magdalene discovered the empty tomb and nearly mistook the resurrected Christ for the gardener (Matthew 28:1–10; John 20:1–18). We don't know exactly when, but at some point Jesus appears to Simon Peter. The Emmaus disciples have had a particularly busy Sunday, for we know they walked seven miles earlier in the day from Jerusalem to Emmaus (see chapter 14 of this book for more details). Little did they know, the stranger who joined them for the walk and a meal was the resurrected Jesus himself. And let us not forget, they walked, or perhaps even ran, seven miles back to Jerusalem to spread the news, "He is alive!" Luke's account is fast-moving, for even as the disciples, no doubt breathless, are reporting to "the eleven" about their experience with Jesus, he appears in their midst with a "mic drop" expression of shalom!

> As they were talking about these things, Jesus himself stood among them, and said to them, "Peace to you!"
>
> Luke 24:36 ESV

Shalom functions as a major descriptor throughout the Bible for salvation, but it centers on the finished work of Jesus Christ. Only in the physical, bodily resurrection of Jesus does the full expression of shalom come true. Jesus used the common greeting, "Shalom to you," but from this moment on, "Shalom to you" means so much more because of his decisive victory over sin and death. Professor George R. Beasley-Murray writes:

> Never had that "common word" [shalom] been so filled with meaning as when Jesus uttered it on Easter evening. All that the prophets had poured into *shalom* as the epitome of the blessings of the kingdom of God had essentially been realized in the redemptive deeds of the incarnate Son of God, "lifted up" for the salvation of the world. His "Shalom!" on Easter evening is the complement of "It is finished" on the cross, for the peace of reconciliation and life from God is now imparted. "Shalom!" accordingly is supremely the Easter greeting.[4]

When you discover the true meaning of shalom, it will transform your life. Jesus is our shalom. In Jesus we experience peace *with* God (Romans 5:1) and the peace *of* God (Colossians 3:15). Jesus established a lasting, eternal peace for us through his death and resurrection, which is available to all on the basis not of works but of faith in him. As pastor Nicky Gumbel says, "Peace is not the absence of trouble, it's the presence of Jesus in the midst of trouble."[5]

Luke and Paul wrote more than half of the New Testament,[6] and *peace* is significant in all of their writings. At various places "peace" and "salvation" are used interchangeably. It is noteworthy that in Luke's gospel and his sequel, the book of Acts, the word *peace* appears thirteen and seven times respectively. Luke's gospel is written for a Roman audience. The peace of Rome (Pax Romana) or, more specifically, the peace of Augustus, was the great lie of the first century. Clearly, Luke is writing about true and lasting peace found not in Augustus or Rome, but in Jesus, the Lord of all. Luke records Zacharias's prophecy of peace: "Because of the tender mercy of our God, with which the Sunrise (the Messiah) from on high will dawn and visit us, to shine upon those who sit in darkness and the shadow of death, to guide our feet [in a straight line] into the way of peace" (Luke 1:78–79 AMP). The backdrop to this prophecy uttered by Zacharias, John the Baptist's father, is Isaiah 59:8: "They do not know the way of peace" (AMP). In other words, without Jesus we do not know the way of peace. It is unattainable.

In the magisterial work of Romans, Paul's letter is bookended with the word *peace* (1:7; 16:20). His one mention of Satan in Romans comes with this victorious promise: "The God of peace will soon crush Satan under your feet" (16:20). Elsewhere in Romans, Paul writes that we serve "the God of hope" who fills us with "all joy and peace as [we] trust in him" (15:13 NIV). In Ephesians, Paul utilizes the first three chapters to share with believers all that is theirs in Jesus Christ: "But now in Christ Jesus you who once were far off have been brought near by the blood of Christ. For He Himself is our peace" (2:13–14 NKJV). Also in Ephesians, Paul states that the gospel itself is "the gospel of peace" (6:15), and that Jesus "came and preached peace to you who were far away, and peace to those who were near" (2:17 NASB 1995). And in

2 Thessalonians, Paul prays for the peace of fellow saints: "Now may the Lord of peace himself give you peace at all times and in every way. The Lord be with all of you" (3:16 NIV).

Paul uses the phrase "the God of peace" six times, and as we have seen, God's peace is the antidote to anxiety (see Philippians 4:9). We serve "the God of hope" who fills us with "all joy and peace as [we] trust in him" (Romans 15:13 NIV). Isaiah 9:6–7 tells of the coming Messiah King known as the Prince of Peace:

> His name will be called
> "Wonderful Counselor, Mighty God,
>   Everlasting Father, Prince of Peace."
> Of the increase of his government and of peace
>   there will be no end.

Jesus established peace for us! Jesus' peace is an *objective* reality, and the *subjective* feeling of peace will come as we allow Christ to be established in our hearts through communion with him in his Word.

The night before Jesus was crucified, he told his disciples, "Peace I leave with you; my peace I give to you, not as the world gives do I give to you. Let not your hearts be troubled, neither let them be afraid" (John 14:27). The double use of "peace" in Jesus' last words is inspiring.

Jesus gives something the world (i.e., Vanity Fair) cannot give: *peace*. Temporary "peace," the only peace the world offers, is circumstantial at best. And notice Jesus' words: "I leave with you . . . I give to you." He gives us a gift, a gift called peace. This is a "Christ-given serenity,"[7] and you can have it right now in Jesus.

We Live on Promises, Not Explanations

To experience peace, we must learn to live by faith in the promises and character of God. No one lives by having faith in explanations.

All of the heroes of the Scriptures lived by faith in the promises of God. Faith is taking God at his Word, not asking him for an explanation. That doesn't mean we cannot ask God, "Why?" But in my experience, God wants us to trust him in the moment, rather than asking for an explanation.

When God promises shalom—peace *that passes all understanding*—he means it. As a father of five, my children often want to know why they cannot do certain activities. Even if I explained the ramifications of some dangerous activity, they would likely still not understand why they can't do it. In those moments, my children trust me and the promise I make to them: "Follow me . . . don't do this . . . do that . . ." The point is, they trust the promise, not the explanation. If you are injured, you may not even care how the injury specifically occurred (an explanation). Rather, you want the promise of the doctor for when you will be better. We live life on promises, not explanations. The great Bible teacher Warren Wiersbe discussed this point at length in his Genesis commentary, both in the preface and his comments on Genesis 22:3–5:

> Living by faith means obeying God's Word in spite of feelings, circumstances, or consequences. It means holding on to God's truth no matter how heavy the burden or how dark the day, knowing that He is working out His perfect plan. *It means living by promises and not by explanations.*[8]

One particularly challenging comment Wiersbe made is this: "Faith does not demand explanations; faith rests on promises."[9] This reminds me that as I pray for peace and shalom, I can trust God to bring his peace. It does not mean I should expect a full explanation for my trial. Our job is to obey God's Word, his promises, knowing that since God is truth, he can never lie and is fully reliable. Resting in God's promises rather than requiring explanations allows you to stay focused on your calling and priorities, and then moving in the direction of your values. And perhaps God will show you in his time (not yours) why the road bended in your life.

Habakkuk is best known for his powerful statement recorded in 2:4: "The just shall live by his faith" (quoted in Romans 1:17 NKJV; Galatians 3:11; and Hebrews 10:38). Less known is the fact that this same prophet asked God for an explanation in chapter one: "How long, LORD, must I call for help, but you do not listen?" (Habakkuk 1:2 NIV). Habakkuk's calling was to prophecy the doom of Judah days before the invasion of Nebuchadnezzar (605 BC). Of course, he did not realize what God was doing. Daniel and his three friends would be taken captive in Nebuchadnezzar's sacking of Jerusalem, and you are likely familiar with the events that followed in Daniel's life. Nevertheless, I am quite certain Habakkuk was not excited about his prophetic assignment.

So how did the Lord respond to Habakkuk's request for an explanation? "'Look at the nations and watch—and be utterly amazed. For I am going to do something in your days that you would not believe, even if you were told'" (1:5 NIV). Though perplexed, Habakkuk then learned to trust God because of who God *is*. Interestingly, God gave Habakkuk a vision of what he was doing, and Habakkuk nearly collapsed (see 3:16). Only then did Habakkuk utter that great faith statement of the Bible: We have to live by faith!

Habakkuk chapter three, according to Dr. Charles Ryrie, is "a great psalm of praise, scarcely equaled anywhere else in the Old Testament.[10] Here is the progression: 1) Lord, I need an explanation. God replies that Habakkuk can't handle the explanation; 2) I will live by faith; and 3) praise erupts! All of Habakkuk's confidence was in the Lord God: "The Sovereign LORD is my strength; he makes my feet like the feet of a deer, he enables me to tread on the heights" (3:19 NIV).

Salvation (Shalom/Peace) Is the Gift of God, in Jesus, through Faith

We experience the peace of God when we have peace with God. How do we have peace with God? Through faith in Jesus Christ and his finished work on the cross on our behalf. The gospel is good news. Jesus died in our place. Another way to understand this fact is that he died *instead* of us. Jesus' death and resurrection fully paid for our sin debt, not only appeasing God's wrath for sin, but also making the way of complete and total forgiveness available. Furthermore, Jesus lived a perfectly righteous life. Second Corinthians 5:21 clearly states a beautiful exchange happens when we trust in Jesus Christ as our Savior: "God made him who had no sin to be sin for us, so that in him we might become the righteousness of God" (NIV). As author and preacher Mike Gendron says, "God treated Jesus as if he lived your life and mine, so he could treat you and me as if we lived the life of Jesus. That's the glorious gospel of grace."[11]

Sound too good to be true? If so, that's the point. You are beginning to understand the concept of grace.

Grace.

Grace and peace.

Grace, peace, and mercy.

No wonder these words find themselves throughout the cut and thrust of the New Testament. The teaching that salvation is conditioned solely on faith appears over two hundred times in the New Testament. Works are a grace-killing element. The only thing you can bring to the cross has already been brought there: your sins. Have you placed your trust in Jesus Christ for your forgiveness of sin and eternal life with him? You can do that right now. Just believe.

Back to Habakkuk 2:4: "The just shall live by his faith" (NKJV). We begin our relationship with God through Jesus Christ in faith, and we continue to live the Christian life by faith. Hebrews 10:39

cites Habakkuk 2:4 as a clear call to continue in the faith: "But we are not of those who shrink back to destruction, but of those who have faith to the preserving of the soul" (NASB 1995). God's Holy Word says we have been "granted . . . His precious and magnificent promises" (2 Peter 1:4 NASB 1995). What does God want us to do? We must continuously trust him. With God there are no hopeless situations, and that is why we can be assured of his peace that passes all understanding and will guard our hearts and our minds through Christ Jesus.

As we have seen in this chapter and throughout the book, we cannot become the follower of Jesus he wants us to be if our faith is not tested along the journey.[12] God will either deliver us from the problem we are facing, or he will deliver us through the problem, but we can always be assured of his presence and peace in the problem. As Col. R.B. Thieme writes in his work *Christian, at Ease!*, "God's Word never says, 'God helps those who help themselves,' rather, God helps the helpless."[13] Isaiah promises, "He gives strength to the weary and increases the power of the weak" (40:29 NIV). Our faith, says Col. Thieme, "should be an ever-present, positive, moment-by-moment trust in the power of God to handle our 'catastrophes.'"[14]

So, we have a choice to continually make as followers of Jesus: Will we live in shalom or fear? Will we unleash shalom in our life, mixing the promises of God with faith in both God's character and God's promises? Or will we live in anxiety? The promise of Jesus is sure and steadfast: "I have said these things to you, that in me you may have peace. In the world you will have tribulation. But take heart; I have overcome the world" (John 16:33 ESV).

So, I say to you, *Shalom! Shalom! Shalom!* Don't settle for the lies of Vanity Fair that steal the peace in your life.

PART 2

LIVING AND APPLYING SHALOM IN GOD'S WORLD

Vulnerability Is the New Superpower

Christians are the only group that shoots their wounded." I will never forget this devastating comment from someone who was deeply hurt in a moment of vulnerability gone wrong. While it is not my aim here to respond to this comment or its projection on the history and influence of Christianity, I do want to recognize the inherent risk of what I am laying out in this chapter. Being vulnerable—letting someone know you're wounded or allowing others to see your wounds—is a risk, but it is a risk worth taking.

I do not care for clichés; we have too many. As a Bible scholar and exegete (which means I believe the Word of God will always do the work of God), I am not interested in bumper-sticker theology, either. God's Word is inexhaustible and calls us into deep and abiding fellowship with him. Still, I must share a cliché that is both humorous and an indictment of the modern church: "Christians don't gossip; we just share prayer requests." This cuts deep likely because we can probably all call to mind an experience where it proved true. My prayer is that this chapter will call you to a more authentic, refreshing faith fixed on Jesus Christ. Feeble as it may be at times, our faith should be utterly relevant and expressed in God-honoring vulnerability.

———————

Professor J.P. Moreland was a guest on my *Jeremiah Johnston Show*. He and I were in the deep end of the pool discussing his book *Scientism and Secularism* and some of the problems with a rigid adherence to "scientism" rather than "science," when J.P. dropped a vulnerability bomb in the middle of the live, nationally syndicated radio broadcast. Let's set the table with the context. To start with, we were not having a private conversation. After all, this was an evergreen radio broadcast that will be available for a long time in the on-demand world. And who is J.P. Moreland? One respected group recently named him as one of the "The 50 Most Influential Living Philosophers" (Christian or secular).[1] The distinguished professor of philosophy at Biola University has authored and contributed to nearly a hundred books. J.P. Moreland is a Christian thinker, to be sure, and his life, scholarship, and ministry continue to impact thousands of people.

Another important contextual point is that near the end of my show, I almost always ask my guests if they have an "unanswered question" for God. *What would you ask Jesus if you could ask him anything right now?* I was astounded by J.P.'s response: "My unanswered question for God is why he doesn't show up in my life when I feel like it would be in his best interest to show up in that moment." J.P. continued, "I have a genetic predisposition to anxiety and depression from my mother's side of the family. . . . I have experienced two nervous breakdowns. One in 2004, and the other in 2014 caused me to stop teaching for a while. . . . At times I have struggled with debilitating mental illness. Yet, I take refuge in the fact that 28 percent of the psalms are psalms of lament. 'God, I need you!' 'God will you please help me!' 'Where are you God?'"[2]

I was awestruck by J.P.'s display of humility, but more than that, his ability to express vulnerability was at once both stunning and refreshing. I've welcomed dozens of guests to the show and found their responses to our "unanswered question" segment fascinating. But J.P.'s answer certainly was a moment of exemplary clarity. He displayed in a few brief moments what the church needs more today than ever before: *vulnerability*. Again, J.P. Moreland is one of the most respected philosophers and thinkers alive today, specializing in metaphysics, philosophy of the mind, chemistry, and theology, yet he is not immune from struggles with anxiety, depression, and mental illness.

One other important reflection on my discussion with J.P.: I am grateful for his courage to publish books and accept media appearances in focus areas that go beyond his academic research and scholarship. Many Christians in the academic world, due to a variety of reputational pressures, stop short of publicly sharing or publishing in areas related to their personal journey. Why? We do not live in a society that celebrates vulnerability in professional, business, and institutional settings.

In my years spent ministering on topics related to mental wellness (both in live events and our media broadcasts), I have listened to new friends and acquaintances who crave an authentic and vulnerable faith. Conversely, I have heard from many who end up questioning their faith, or even considered abandoning it, because of the combination of two toxic mixtures: 1) the isolation caused by any of the associated mental illnesses, and 2) the church's apparent silence (invulnerability) on issues related to anxiety, depression, and mental illness. So many feel (wrongly) that they suffer alone because they rarely or never personally hear any Christian they respect discuss issues related to depression and anxiety.

In this chapter you will learn important principles, starting with everyone can be vulnerable, *which means you can be vulnerable,* and everyone *should* be vulnerable—it will become your superpower to earning the right to be heard. I truly believe that authentic vulnerability saves, changes, and transforms lives.

Vulnerability Is Defined by Its Risks. Or Is It?

Vulnerability is defined by the risk of being attacked or harmed, either physically or emotionally.[3] The origins of the word date back to the seventeenth-century Latin word *vulnerare*, "to wound." A thesaurus uses "weakness" as a related word. The crowd-sourced Urban Dictionary defines *vulnerable* as what happens when you trust completely, with exposure for someone you trust to do emotional damage or healing. Unfortunately, vulnerability is almost exclusively associated with negative consequences of rejection or judgment. But does vulnerability always result in rejection? Certainly not. Vulnerability deepens relationships, and authentic relationships are marked by transparency and vulnerability. I define Christian vulnerability as "God's strength through my weakness."

Asking for help is vulnerability. Trusting another is vulnerability. Loving someone is vulnerability. Forgiving is vulnerability. Owning up to a mistake and apologizing is vulnerability. Sharing a testimony of how Jesus Christ transformed your life is vulnerability. Yet, a German study published by the American Psychological Association showed we value vulnerability in other people but fear being vulnerable ourselves.[4]

Paul faced this same dilemma in ministering to the church he founded in Corinth. His accusers, the "super-apostles," desired a sparring match with Paul about who was most gifted, powerful, and equipped. Paul instead offers a principle that turns the world's understanding of power on its head: "When I am weak, then I am strong" (2 Corinthians 12:10).[5] Paul's credentials were impressive (in Philippians 3:4–8, he lists seven aspects of his remarkable layers of his Jewish upbringing and education). What's more, Paul had impressive heavenly experiences "in paradise," where he "heard things that cannot be told, which man may not utter" (see 2 Corinthians 12:1–6).[6] In a world of highlight reels, the modern Christian mind may puzzle that Paul did not own these experiences and credentials as his "mark of true apostleship" and authority. Astoundingly, and in a truly countercultural way, Paul points to his "weaknesses" as the true mark of his apostleship. Enter vulnerability.

Christian Vulnerability Is Spirit-Led, Not Manufactured

The Bible presents vulnerability as a necessity of balanced Christian living. We are not vulnerable for vulnerability's sake. All attempts at superficial displays of spirituality should be avoided at all cost. Our vulnerability drives us to greater dependency on Jesus Christ and thereby makes us more effective in representing the presence of Christ to others.

Second Corinthians, written by the apostle Paul, is unusually autobiographical. In a striking statement, he shares about an unanswered prayer: "Three times I pleaded with the Lord to take it away from me" (12:8 NIV), but God said no. In a previous book of mine, *Unanswered*, I expounded on the fact that Paul is often referred to as the Job of the New Testament.[7] Like Job, Paul faced so many problems that his critics and opponents claimed he was not actually an apostle, because it was apparent that God had abandoned him. Paul responded by arguing that his suffering was, in fact, the very mark of his apostleship (see 2 Corinthians 3:1–18). Paul declared, "We do not lose heart" (2 Corinthians 4:1), even though his reality was one of brokenness and suffering—"afflicted in every way, but not crushed" (v. 8).

This section of Paul's letter reminds me of Garth Brooks's top-of-the-charts hit "Unanswered Prayers," where he opines, "Some of God's greatest gifts are unanswered prayers." I think Paul would agree.

So to keep me from becoming conceited because of the surpassing greatness of the revelations, a thorn was given me in the flesh, a messenger of Satan to harass me, to keep me from becoming conceited. Three times I pleaded with the Lord about this, that it should leave me. But he said to me, "My grace is sufficient for you, for my power is made perfect in weakness." Therefore I will boast all the more gladly of my weaknesses, so that the power of Christ may rest upon me. For the sake of Christ, then, I am content with weaknesses, insults, hardships, persecutions, and calamities. For when I am weak, then I am strong.

2 Corinthians 12:7–10 ESV

The Greek word *skolops*, translated as "thorn" above, is the word used for the stake upon which they impaled criminals in Paul's time. Paul's vulnerability—expressed through his dependence on the transforming power of God's grace through Jesus Christ—allows him to glory in his weaknesses. To be even more clear with the original intent, the experiences that scarred Paul, by God's healing and redeeming grace, became his greatest marks of victory: "For I bear on my body the marks of Jesus" (Galatians 6:17).

Again, is there a finer expression of vulnerability by a follower of Jesus than "For when I am weak, then I am strong" (2 Corinthians 12:10)? Where did Paul draw his strength? How did he go from insecurity to security? The answer is that "the power of Christ" is made perfect in weakness (2 Corinthians 12:9).

Make no mistake, the trials and adversity you overcome by God's grace become the perch for your greatest future ministry and spiritual impact. The late Ralph Martin's commentary on 2 Corinthians is one I treasure in my personal library. Martin notes, "Paul exhibits a joyful walk with God undergirded by a firm security in God's grace. So deep-seated is Paul's delight that what he has endured does not compare to what is his in Christ."[8] Indeed, this is a promise we can apply to any problem in our lives. Nothing we endure compares to what we have in Christ. This is the thrust of 2 Corinthians, and it should reverberate in our lives as we seek God today.

Jesus Spoke to Paul during His Most Significant Moment of Vulnerability (and He Will Speak to You, Too)

So where do we go with our pain? How does the healing begin?

So often our pain, hurts, and ailments are emotionally and spiritually paralyzing. Paul was clearly in pain and needed healing. He needed super-strength from above. No doubt he asked others to pray for him. I am sure he confided in friends. We can speculate Paul may have even shared his intense struggle with his accountability group (Barnabas, Silas, and Timothy). What do we know for sure? Paul was vulnerable with God. He went directly to God with his pain and wasn't afraid to be vulnerable. And Paul sought the Lord more than once. It is fascinating to note that in 2 Corinthians 12:8, Paul used the aorist tense (past test) of "pleaded" to describe the fact that he no longer had this prayer request ("I pleaded with the Lord three times" [NKJV]). He didn't even bother praying about it anymore. Why? Jesus spoke to him.

Paul wrote thirteen of the twenty-seven New Testament books. Only "Dr. Luke," with his Luke/Acts sequel, contributed more to the New Testament corpus than Paul. We know of one time (from Paul's writings) that the risen Christ spoke directly to Paul. It is recorded as an answer to Paul's prayer in 2 Corinthians 12:9: "but he [Jesus the Lord] said to me." Ralph Martin suggests, "Paul still hears the echo of this divine oracle."⁹ Martin is correct in thinking that Paul's language—"but he said to me"—is oracular rather than intuitive or a hunch. For example, when someone says, "I felt God was telling me, 'Do the right thing,'" it is usually understood as a sense or leading or intuition, not literally hearing God say something. That's not what Paul is talking about here in

2 Corinthians 12:9. He means that he actually heard God's voice! That's what is meant by oracular; Paul heard an oracle, a word from God.

The nineteenth-century Princeton theologian Charles Hodge wrote:

> "He has said;" the answer was ever sounding in the apostle's ears, and not in his ears only, but in those of all his suffering people from that day to this. Each hears the Lord say, *My grace is sufficient for thee*, ἀρκεῖ σοι ἡ χάρις μου. These words should be engraven on the palm of every believer's hand.[10]

The fascinating point here in highlighting the tenses of both the prayer request and Jesus' answer to Paul is the plain fact that Paul no longer asked God for help to remove the affliction of this thorn in his flesh because the words Jesus spoke to him were as fresh today as they were when he first heard them strengthening his faith: "My grace is sufficient for you" (2 Corinthians 12:9). Even though Paul heard Christ's answer to his many requests in the past, that very answer empowered, even renewed him, today.

Let's also not miss what happens when we take the risk of vulnerability with God. Paul's vulnerability with God led to a powerful experience of God in his life. In other words, there is an experiential faith-link between vulnerability with God and healing from God. Healing was a process in Paul's life. Indeed, he was likely not fully healed, in the sense that his ailment was over. Yet he found God's powerful presence more than enough to meet the need in his life.

So many followers of Jesus mask their pain and are unwilling to take the risk of being vulnerable with God. Guess what? God already knows everything about you! He knows you are struggling. He knows exactly where your pressure points are right now. Why don't you bring them before the Lord? Did you know God knows you better than you know yourself? We don't pray to impress God or inform God. We pray to invite God's presence and power into our lives. In prayer we take on the mind of Christ. The seventeenth-century Puritan thinker Richard Baxter keenly wrote in a treasured hymn, "Christ leads me through no darker rooms than he went through before."[11] You can be sure Jesus knows the weight of your struggle. He's been there. He will carry you through because he is the Lord.

Paul's favorite term for Jesus, indeed, the key name for Jesus in the New Testament, is "the Lord." In one form or another, Paul used it more than two hundred times in his thirteen epistles. Elsewhere I have written about the emergence and importance of the term "the Lord's Day," which is astounding considering it was not Saturday and the first Christians were Jewish. It's also helpful to remember the importance of praying directly to Jesus (see Acts 2:21; 7:59; 9:14, 21; 22:16; 1 Thessalonians 3:12–13; 1 Corinthians 1:2; 16:22).

How does vulnerability become our superpower to reach others? I stand in agreement with Martin's comment on Paul's thorn-in-my-flesh statement in 2 Corinthians 12:7: "Because of his [Paul's] weakness he became a powerful instrument for God."[12] No one has arrived in the faith. Based on that same verse, the messenger of Satan was likely still buffeting Paul as he wrote to his beloved church family. Yet, Paul found his strength in God and was able to carry the day in ministry and life. The problem became Paul's (super)power because his source of strength was no longer himself but God. God's perpetual gift grace in both Paul and our spiritual lives never runs dry. His grace stands as a mighty rushing river, able to move us through any problem, adversity, and trial, no matter spiritual, physical, emotional, or mental.

Power is brought to fulfillment simultaneously in weakness when we depend on Christ. In Paul's writing, *power* and *grace* are synonyms. I find the NLT rendering particularly insightful: "My grace is all you need. My power works best in weakness"

(2 Corinthians 12:9). Paul states and then restates Christ's answer to his prayer:

Jesus' direct reply to Paul's prayer	My grace is sufficient for you, for my power is made perfect in weakness (2 Corinthians 12:9)
Paul's reformulates[13] the Word of the Lord to him	For when I am weak, then I am strong (v. 10)

God had answered Paul's prayer of vulnerability at some point in the past, and his answer—and character—still held true and continued to strengthen Paul.

> He gives power to the faint,
>   and to him who has no might he increases strength.
> Even youths shall faint and be weary,
>   and young men shall fall exhausted;
> but they who wait for the LORD shall renew their strength,
>   they shall mount up with wings like eagles,
> they shall run and not be weary,
>   they shall walk and not faint.
>
> Isaiah 40:29–31

Back to our point of thanking God for unanswered prayer: Paul asked God to remove a problem, God answered differently than asked for, and he blessed Paul with something far greater than removing his problem.

Vulnerability Will Always Lead Me to Glory in Christ, Not in My Struggle

A significant point is implied in the fact that Paul does not share specific details beyond 1) there was an immense struggle with a thorn in his flesh, and 2) it was a messenger of Satan attacking him. Much to the disappointment of many commentators, pastors, and Bible students, Paul gives no further detail about his struggle. Rather, Paul glories in the fact that Christ's strength is literally made perfect in and through this particular weakness.

Every time we rely on our strength, we will fail. This is Paul's point. When we allow God's power to meet us in our weakness, we are most effective. Indeed, we accomplish so much more when God leaves us with a limp! So, as we reach out to a hurting world with the superpower of vulnerability, let us never forget to glory in Christ and not in our afflictions.

I get uneasy when a follower of Jesus speaks more about their struggles than God's delivering, redeeming power and presence. Yes, we can (and should) share where we have struggled, but we shouldn't park there. As we prayerfully consider being vulnerable, we do so always in a God-honoring way. We are careful to share only what the Spirit of God leads us to say. Often, before I speak at a major event or for a Bible study, or before being interviewed on a media program, I will ask God to help me to share only what he desires in a way that always gives him the glory. We glory in our weakness only when Christ is enthroned and glorified by our walk with him in the adversity of life.

The Vulnerability Rule for Believers: When I Am Weak, Then I Am Powerful

When is the last time you bragged about your problems and weaknesses? Probably never, right? I cannot recall a Bible study I led or attended where anyone relished in their difficult issues. But maybe we are doing the Christian life wrong.

Paul says we "rejoice in our sufferings" (Romans 5:3 ESV) and "I delight in weaknesses, in insults, in hardships, in persecutions, in difficulties" (2 Corinthians 12:10 NIV). It appears Paul unlocked an ancient principle of the Christian life that is all but lost in our modern times, when Christian leaders are heard because of their following, charisma, or abilities, rather than the true credential of suffering for the name of Christ. When a follower of Christ humbly admits their weaknesses, immediately Christ's own power begins to work in their life. Paul was not weak because he was backslidden or uncommitted, or because of unconfessed sin. He was weak because he endured hardship for the sake of Christ. Yet Paul's faith was unmoved; he relied on God's grace pumping through his spirit and he accepted his afflictions.

At this point, we must ask ourselves, what affliction(s) have we endured for or on behalf of Jesus Christ? Paul said he counted everything outside of knowing Christ as "loss" and "rubbish" (Philippians 3:8 ESV). In other words, Paul did not want to see any part of his life outside of Christ, even adversity!

Vulnerability Opens New Opportunities God Desires for Us

We live in a world full of artificiality and social media highlight reels. In a time when we are supposedly more connected, it is more difficult to relate to one another. This sad fact causes much pain. We believe the lies that we are disqualified or perhaps not "gifted enough" for God to use us for anything, let alone have a special purpose. Yet, a tremendous payoff in studying 2 Corinthians 12:1–10 is understanding that our weaknesses and struggles become the megaphone for God not only to show himself strong in our lives, but to take us places we never imagined while being in communion with him and used by him.

In recognizing our own vulnerability, we become better Christians, parents, citizens, students, disciples, and people. Not implementing or allowing for vulnerability leads to further isolation and artificiality. Vulnerability, and the humility that comes with it, is God's expressway to releasing his power in your life. Why resist? One insightful commentator noted Paul's understanding of God's power as a "daily new gift" coming to believers through the work of Christ's power in their lives.[14] Could it be that the weakness you are experiencing is God's way of molding you into the Christian he wants you to be?

One final lesson from Paul's vulnerability is insightful: the timing. When he said, "When I am weak, then I am powerful," what did *when* actually mean? The force of the Greek "when" [lit. ὅταν, a temporal particle rather than ὅτε] is more open-ended because Paul's "weaknesses, insults, hardships" (2 Corinthians 12:10) and "thorn . . . in the flesh" (2 Corinthians 12:7) were constant. Therefore, he was the perpetual recipient of the personal power of Jesus: "To this end I strenuously contend with all the energy Christ so powerfully works in me" (Colossians 1:29 NIV). If you have a lifelong, debilitating struggle, you are in good company. So did Paul. Rely on God's grace. Press into God's love and care for you, and watch his power fill and transform you.

Advocate Vulnerability for Others

In 2008, Dr. Eric Manheimer made the decision to die. Squamous cell carcinoma of the throat—a pea-sized lesion first—had spread to the fifty-eight-year-old's lymph nodes. His medical training had him believing there was little hope, and he refused further chemotherapy and radiation treatment. But as he wrote later, his wife, Diana, saved him from himself. He shared his experience three years later in a *New York Times* op-ed, and cited a study that found that physicians might recommend different treatments for their patients than they would for themselves.[15] A layer of care was missing with most doctors and treatment plans: being vulnerable with patients and understanding their sense of vulnerability. When Manheimer got cancer, "I wasn't a doctor anymore," he wrote, "I was a patient."

> During one particularly desperate hospitalization, after receiving blood transfusions and a drug to stimulate my white cells, I decided that I had had enough. I refused further radiation and

chemotherapy. I lay in my bed and watched the events around me—the distress of my family, the helplessness of my doctors—without anxiety, comfortable that I had made the correct decision. My doctors couldn't override it or persuade me to change my mind, but, luckily, my wife, Diana, could and did. From my mental cocoon in the hospital bed, I could sense Diana at my side. "You're going to finish the treatment," she said softly. I did not have the energy, or perhaps the will, to disagree. She wheeled me down herself to finish my radiation treatments in the basement of the hospital. My dreams of dying were not the products of anxious moments of terror. The life force had simply slipped away and made me ready to die. It had also rendered me incapable of making the right decision for myself. My disease was treatable and the odds were favorable. . . . If anything, it's that recognition of vulnerability as well as expertise that makes me a better doctor today.[16]

Dr. Manheimer was cured. His lesson proved profound: vulnerability, along with expertise, is essential for excellent medical care.

You may not recognize Dr. Manheimer's name, but his personal story and reputation for loving patients as the medical director of Bellevue Hospital Center (America's oldest public hospital, located in New York City, since 1736) captured the hearts and minds of Hollywood. A little over a year after writing his compelling op-ed, Manheimer wrote a book, *Twelve Patients: Life and Death at Bellevue Hospital.* Four networks were interested in developing Manheimer's experiences and approach to care into a television show, but NBC won the rights, and *New Amsterdam* premiered and has enjoyed a multi-season run.[17] Dr. Manheimer serves as producer on the series to ensure its integrity and accuracy. Those who have watched the program or read Manheimer's book are arrested by the love, care, and compassion exemplified in his care of each individual patient. What is the X factor in Manheimer's approach? Again, vulnerability paired with expertise.

Often, we need others to save us from ourselves. We need the compassion of another image-bearer, like Diana, to whisper in our ears and into our hearts, "You will make it. You will get through this. When you are weak, you are powerful in Christ."

Let me say to you, whatever you are facing, you *will* make it. You *will* get through this. In Christ, you are more than a conqueror.

7

God Is My Shield

Have you ever experienced God's protection in your life? Would a situation have turned out differently without God's intervention? Numerous examples in my life come to mind. There's no doubt God protected our triplets in a high-risk pregnancy. God has also protected me from myself by offering wisdom in the face of poor decisions. And I am certain God has protected me many more times, of which I am still (temporarily) unaware.

One of my earliest memories of divine protection and intervention was a car accident I experienced as a seventh grader while traveling with my dad. Following a long weekend of dynamic evangelistic ministry near Trenton, New Jersey, we were driving back to the motel, hoping to make it in time to get dinner at the Big Boy restaurant (remember those?). I remember noticing how dark it was outside. Dad and I were discussing the great way in which God had worked that weekend, when suddenly, almost out of nowhere, we collided with another vehicle (almost head-on). Our rental car spun around and around, and the airbags were deployed, sending oozing powder everywhere. We finally came to a screeching stop against a median, and an eerie stillness filled the vehicle. I began to panic. My father looked dead. His head was awkwardly leaning against the headrest, his mouth was open, and he wasn't moving. I am not afraid to admit that I screamed. It felt like a bad dream, even a nightmare. The powder from the airbags made me think our car was about to explode.

I reached over and tried to wake Dad, but he was unresponsive. Then I tried getting out, but my door was completely jammed. I couldn't open it with all of my teenage strength and adrenaline. Just then, Dad's door flung open, and an African American man pulled him out of the car. He then pulled me out. Outside, my focus was on my father, who was lying motionless on his back in the grassy median. Then, like a gift from heaven, it began to rain lightly. My dad finally jostled awake as the sprinkles landed on his eyelids. "Jer, are we in Alaska?" he mumbled. "Are we in Alaska, Jer? What happened? Are we okay?" His confusion frightened me—two weeks earlier, he had preached in Anchorage—but I learned later that Dad was concussed. He had hit his head so hard that he had lost his short-term memory.

Relieved and thankful my dad was alive, I suddenly remembered the man who had rescued us. *Where is he?* I looked all around. I didn't see him speaking to the officers and EMTs who were now on the scene. He was gone, almost like he had vanished.

I believe with all of my heart I experienced an "angel unaware" that night. God was my shield. He had protected us from a far-worse outcome. The book of Hebrews says, "Do not neglect to show hospitality to strangers, for thereby some have entertained angels unawares" (13:2). We never returned to the motel. We were forced to stay overnight in the hospital for observation. But God faithfully protected and cared for us.

When my wife, Audrey, and I first began in ministry, we shared this story, and I asked those in our Bible study class to write if they had ever experienced God's tangible deliverance or experienced angelic assistance. We received the equivalent of a small book of tremendous stories of God's faithful protection and intervention.

One reason we can experience God's shalom and happiness in our lives is because of God's divine protection. Divine protection is a theme in the Bible that often goes unmentioned. We are used to hearing about forgiveness and salvation—usually in reference to the future—but we don't often hear about how God protects his people in the here and now. The Bible, in fact, has much to say about this important topic. Indeed, from beginning to end, our Triune God promises to protect and save those who trust him.

God as a Protective Shield

In the book of Genesis—the first book in the Bible—God initiates his redemptive, saving work by calling Abram and promising to give him a land and to make him the father of a multitude of people (Genesis 12:1–3). God sends him into a new land, a land of strangers and a land of danger. Abram is but one man, and is vulnerable. Without the support of extended family and familiar surroundings, Abram faces the unknown. It is in that uncertain, fearful situation that God appears to the patriarch and gives him a word of assurance that changes the course of human history:

> The word of the LORD came to Abram in a vision, "Do not be afraid, Abram; I am your shield; your reward shall be very great."
>
> Genesis 15:1 NRSV

I want to draw attention to the word *shield* that appears above (and also in Scriptures highlighted below). The Hebrew word is *māgēn*. It's a great word, and it is not surprising that today it is a popular name for Jewish men, especially in Israel. In Genesis 15, God promised Abram that, like a shield, he would protect him from potential threats and enemies. Indeed, God did protect the patriarch and fulfill all of the promises made to him. Abram, whose name was later changed to Abraham ("Father of a Multi-tude"), came to reside in the land that today is known as Israel. He had sons born to him, including Isaac, the promised heir, and acquired honor and respect throughout the region. Today, Abraham has millions of genetic descendants (half of whom live in Israel), and almost one half of the human population—religiously and spiritually speaking—are his descendants.

God did not protect Abraham only; he protected his descendants. God promised Moses and the people of Israel, after they had departed from Egypt, "Behold, I send an angel before you, to guard you on the way and to bring you to the place which I have prepared" (Exodus 23:20). God fulfilled his promise, protecting the not-always-obedient and not-always-grateful Israel in their wilderness journey. Shortly before his death and shortly before Israel entered the Promised Land, Moses said to God's people, "Happy are you, O Israel! Who is like you, a people saved by the LORD, the **shield** of your help, and the sword of your triumph!" (Deuteronomy 33:29, emphasis mine).

The amazing story of Israel's exodus from Egypt—the sojourn in the wilderness—and the successful entry into and settlement in the Promised Land became sacred and served as a template for faith for the people of Israel for generations. This is why the psalmist can cry out, "O LORD, protect us, guard us" (Psalm 12:7) and "Our soul waits for the LORD; he is our help and **shield**" (Psalm 33:20, emphasis mine). In reference to their unknown future, the prophet Zechariah promises that "The LORD of hosts will protect them" (Zechariah 9:15).

No one more than David gave greater expression to the protective presence and power of God. Threatened on all sides, David confesses, "The LORD is my rock, my fortress, and my deliverer, my God, my rock, in whom I take refuge, my **shield** and the horn of my salvation, my stronghold and my refuge, my savior; you save me from violence. . . . This God—his way is perfect; the promise of the LORD proves true; he is a **shield** for all who take refuge in him. . . . You have given me the **shield** of your salvation, and your help has made me great" (2 Samuel 22:2–3, 31, 36 NRSV, emphasis mine). Three times in this song David refers to God's shield-like protection. God saved David, and the song he sang in 2 Samuel 22 is now found in the book of Psalms in Psalm 18.

The theme of God's protection appears many more times in the Psalter. Some of the songs were written by David; some were written by other Israelites who had placed their trust in the Lord. When David's own son turned against him, and David has to flee, he sings: "You, O LORD, are a **shield** about me, my glory, and the lifter of my head. . . . I will not be afraid of many thousands of people who have set themselves against me all round" (Psalm 3:3, 6 ESV, emphasis mine). David appeals to God, "Oh guard my life, and deliver me; let me not be put to shame, for I take refuge in thee" (Psalm 25:20). David again confesses: "The LORD is my strength and my **shield**; in him my heart trusts; so I am helped, and my heart exults, and with my song I give thanks to him" (Psalm 28:7, emphasis mine). When threatened by a vengeful King Saul, David knows he can call out to God: "Deliver me from my enemies, O my God, protect me from those who rise up against me, deliver me from those who work evil" (Psalm 59:1–2).

God protected his prophets, too. Summoned to appear before an angry king, Elijah hears the assurance of God: "'Go down with him; do not be afraid of him.' So he arose and went down with him to the king" (2 Kings 1:15). In the face of the threat of Assyrian invasion, God comforts Isaiah with his powerful presence, enabling the prophet to declare: "Behold, God is my salvation; I will trust, and will not be afraid; for the LORD GOD is my strength and my song, and he has become my salvation" (Isaiah 12:2). When the Assyrian king threatens King Hezekiah and mocks the God of Israel, Isaiah assures the king: "Thus says the LORD: Do not be afraid because of the words that you have heard, with which the servants of the king of Assyria have reviled me" (2 Kings 19:6). Days later the Assyrian army was decimated with pestilence. The Assyrian king fled, but was later assassinated (2 Kings 19:35–37).

One of the most moving psalms that gives expression to God's protection of his people is Psalm 91. It is well worth citing this psalm in its entirety.

> He who dwells in the shelter of the Most High, who
>   abides in the shadow of the Almighty,
> will say to the LORD, "My refuge and my fortress; my
>   God, in whom I trust."
> For he will deliver you from the snare of the fowler and
>   from the deadly pestilence;
> he will cover you with his pinions, and under his wings
>   you will find refuge; his faithfulness is a **shield** and
>   buckler.
> You will not fear the terror of the night, nor the arrow
>   that flies by day,
> nor the pestilence that stalks in darkness, nor the
>   destruction that wastes at noonday.
> A thousand may fall at your side, ten thousand at your
>   right hand; but it will not come near you.
> You will only look with your eyes and see the recompense
>   of the wicked.
> Because you have made the LORD your refuge, the Most
>   High your habitation,
> no evil shall befall you, no scourge come near your tent.
> For he will give his angels charge of you to guard you in all
>   your ways.
> On their hands they will bear you up, lest you dash your
>   foot against a stone.
> You will tread on the lion and the adder, the young lion
>   and the serpent you will trample under foot.
> Because he cleaves to me in love, I will deliver him; I will
>   protect him, because he knows my name.
> When he calls to me, I will answer him; I will be with him
>   in trouble, I will rescue him and honor him.

> With long life I will satisfy him, and show him my
> salvation. (emphasis mine)

Early on, Psalm 91 became very popular and was often cited in prayers for protection from evil and in prayers for healing. In the Aramaic paraphrase, which emerged in the Aramaic-speaking synagogues of Israel before and during the time of Jesus, Psalm 91 came to be understood as offering protection against evil spirits. Indeed, it is believed that the psalm contains David's words of advice and assurance for his son Solomon (esp. in vv. 2–3, 9), who himself became well known for composing charms and songs that could drive away evil spirits. A few of the verses of Psalm 91 in Aramaic read as follows (vv. 5, 6, 10, with italics indicating the changes):

> You will not fear the terror of the *demons that go about in*
> the night, nor the arrow *of the angel of death that he*
> *shoots* in the day,
> nor the *death* that stalks in darkness, nor the *company of*
> *demons* that *destroy* at noonday. . . .
> The Lord of the world responded, and this is what he
> said: "No evil shall befall you, no scourge *or demons*
> shall come near your tent."

Parts of and sometimes all of Psalm 91 appear in amulets that ancient people wore, hoping God would protect them from evil. Magic scrolls, bowls, and metal foils and tablets quote this psalm in the hope that demons and sickness would be driven away. It is for this reason that Satan himself, when he tempted Jesus in the wilderness, appealed to this psalm to convince Jesus that he would suffer no harm if he threw himself from the pinnacle of the temple in Jerusalem:

> Then the devil took him to the holy city, and set him on the pinnacle
> of the temple, and said to him, "If you are the Son of God, throw

yourself down; for it is written, '*He will give his angels charge of you,*' and 'On their hands they will bear you up, lest you strike your foot against a stone.'" Jesus said to him, "Again it is written, 'You shall not tempt the Lord your God.'"

Matthew 4:5–7, italics added

Jesus knew, of course, that his Father in heaven would protect him and empower him to accomplish his mission and will. He didn't need the devil's help, and he certainly didn't need the devil to explain Scripture to him. (Note: in Luke's version, the quotation of Psalm 91:11, italicized above, reads more fully: "He will give his angels charge of you, to guard you" [4:10].) Having experienced firsthand God's protective presence, Jesus taught his disciples about it. They learned this teaching well and gave expression to it in their preaching and writings, which eventually became the New Testament.

God in Christ Continues to Protect His Children

When the disciples returned from their mission of preaching, they reported to Jesus:

"Lord, even the demons are subject to us in your name!" And he said to them, "I saw Satan fall like lightning from heaven. Behold, I have given you authority to tread upon serpents and scorpions, and over all the power of the enemy; and nothing shall hurt you. Nevertheless do not rejoice in this, that the spirits are subject to you; but rejoice that your names are written in heaven."

Luke 10:17–20

This is a remarkable exchange. Jesus had told the disciples that they would be able to heal and cast out evil spirits (Matthew 10:1; Mark 6:7; Luke 9:1), but to experience it was something else. Their power over evil spirits was evidence of what Jesus tells them that he saw "Satan fall like lightning from heaven." With Satan cast down, his evil allies were weakened and could more easily be defeated. Interpreters think Jesus was alluding to Isaiah's famous oracle, in which the prophet of old declared: "How you are fallen from heaven, O Day Star, son of Dawn! How you are cut down to the ground" (Isaiah 14:12 ESV).

In Greco-Roman thinking, a flash of lightning was an omen of defeat in battle or regime change (e.g., Suetonius, *Divus Augustus* 94.4: a lightning strike signified the coming rule of Emperor Augustus). That's what happened during Jesus' ministry: Satan lost his grip on humanity; he was dethroned and bit the dust. A new sheriff is in town!

Jesus has more to say. He tells his disciples that he has given them "authority to tread upon serpents and scorpions, and over all the power of the enemy; and nothing shall hurt you" (Luke 10:19). Interpreters think these "serpents and scorpions" refer to evil spirits, and that Jesus is actually alluding to Psalm 91 (esp. v. 13), a psalm, as discussed above, understood to offer protection from Satan and evil spirits. A text written a century or so before the ministry of Jesus alludes to Psalm 91:13 with an explicit understanding that it is in reference to Satan (aka Beliar) and his evil spirit allies: "Beliar will be bound by him, and he will give authority to his children to trample upon the evil spirits" (*Testament of Levi* 18:12). That's what Jesus and his disciples were doing in their ministry: walking all over the devil and the evil spirits. Note, too, that the *Testament of Levi* says that the devil "will be bound by him" (that is, bound by the coming redeemer). That's another match for what Jesus has done in his ministry: He has bound the strong man (the devil) and has plundered his house (see Mark 3:27).

Jesus empowered his disciples during their ministry together, but what will happen when he is no longer with his disciples? Jesus knows that in his absence his disciples will be afraid and uncertain. So shortly before his arrest, he prays for them. He prays aloud, which was the Jewish custom, and so in effect gives his disciples his final words, which in the Gospel of John are known as the High Priestly Prayer.

Jesus "lifted up his eyes to heaven" and prayed (John 17:1). In the course of this prayer, Jesus mentions his disciples several times, asking God to protect them. Here are three verses from the passage that I think are especially important:

> And now I am no more in the world, but they are in the world, and I am coming to thee. Holy Father, keep them in thy name, which thou hast given me, that they may be one, even as we are one (v. 11).
>
> While I was with them, I kept them in thy name, which thou hast given me; I have guarded them, and none of them is lost (v. 12).
>
> I do not pray that thou shouldst take them out of the world, but that thou shouldst keep them from the evil one (v. 15).

In this prayer, Jesus asks his Father in heaven to protect his disciples. He asks them to be kept in his name (see v. 11). The point here is that Jesus wants his disciples to be kept from discouragement and from abandonment of their mission. To be "kept" can also mean to be protected, which in the prayer refers to being kept "from the evil one" (v. 15), that is, Satan, the very evil being that tried to tempt Jesus and derail his ministry before it even got started. Having failed to ruin Jesus, the devil will do his best to ruin the ministry of Jesus' disciples. He's been at it ever since.

The disciples have also been kept by Jesus himself. In verse 12, he uses the word "guarded," which in the verb form literally means to keep in lockup. Jesus tells his heavenly Father that he has acted as a guard in protecting his disciples; only Judas Iscariot, the betrayer, was lost. With his departure at hand, it is God's turn to watch over his disciples, to "keep them from the evil one." The evil one is, of course, Satan himself, who from the very beginning of Jesus' ministry has tried in vain to ruin Jesus. That he will try to ruin the disciples and wreck the church is only to be expected.

In John 10:28, Jesus gives the tremendous promise: "and I give them eternal life, and they shall never perish, and no one shall snatch them out of my hand." The word *snatch* is a term of violence, similar to a predator. Jesus, our shield, protects us from the great enemy, who tries to seize us. Also reflected in the promise of Jesus' protection is the wonderful fact of his eternal hold, his protection over us. The great Bible scholar Leon Morris, reflecting on Jesus' words in John 10:28, said, "It is one of the precious things about the Christian faith that our continuance in eternal life depends not on our feeble hold on Christ, but on his firm grip on us. We should notice that the teaching of this verse is not that believers will be saved from all earthly disaster, but that they will be saved, no matter what earthly disaster may befall them."[1]

The Holy Spirit Shields Us

This is why Jesus in his earlier "Farewell Discourse" (John 14–16), which I discussed in chapter 2, promised his disciples the advent of a Comforter or Counselor, which is none other than the Holy Spirit. This Counselor will take the place of Jesus. Here are four important verses:

> I will pray the Father, and he will give you another Counselor, to be with you for ever. (John 14:16)

> The Counselor, the Holy Spirit, whom the Father will send in my name, he will teach you all things, and bring to your remembrance all that I have said to you. (John 14:26)

> But when the Counselor comes, whom I shall send to you from the Father, even the Spirit of truth, who proceeds from the Father, he will bear witness to me. (John 15:26)

Nevertheless I tell you the truth: it is to your advantage that I go away, for if I do not go away, the Counselor will not come to you; but if I go, I will send him to you. (John 16:7)

The word *counselor* can also be translated as "advocate," sometimes in a legal sense, much like an attorney who has his client's interests in mind. We see this in 1 John, where the writer says, "My little children, I am writing this to you so that you may not sin; but if any one does sin, we have an advocate with the Father, Jesus Christ the righteous" (1 John 2:1). The noun form of "Counselor" comes from the verb *parakalein*, which literally means "to be called alongside." That is what a counselor is: one who is summoned to the side of a person who needs advice, encouragement, and direction.

In John 14:26, Jesus identifies the Counselor as the Holy Spirit, and in 15:26 as the "Spirit of truth." The Holy Spirit will act as Counselor and will guide and teach the disciples. He will bring to their remembrance what Jesus has taught them. He will also "bear witness" to Jesus. The Holy Spirit will, moreover, protect the disciples; and they will need protection. For the disciples of Jesus will not only face persecution, as Jesus warns (John 15:20; 16:33), they will also face many challenges in leading the new movement, the church.

The promised Counselor will also strengthen the disciples, for they will face hardship. Jesus warned his disciples: "If they persecuted me, they will persecute you" (John 15:20; cf. John 5:16, where Jesus is persecuted for having healed someone on the Sabbath). The word "persecute" (*diōkein*) appears several times in the New Testament. In his second letter to the Christians of Corinth, Paul remarks that he and other apostles are "persecuted, but not forsaken; struck down, but not destroyed" (2 Corinthians 4:9). In prison and facing death, Paul says to Timothy, "Indeed all who desire to live a godly life in Christ Jesus will be persecuted" (2 Timothy 3:12). Such persecution did not come as a surprise to the apostles. After all, Jesus had warned his followers that they would be persecuted in proclaiming the gospel (e.g., Matthew 10:23; 23:34). Again, this is why Jesus speaks of it in his Farewell Discourse, where he assures his disciples: "I have said this to you, that in me you may have peace. In the world you have tribulation; but be of good cheer, I have overcome the world" (John 16:33). Despite the tribulation and persecution, the disciples will have peace, knowing that Jesus has been victorious.

Come what may, the end is certain. There, we do not need to be fearful. We can be effective witnesses and live abundant lives in Jesus Christ. Knowing that God is our shield (our *māgēn*) is directly connected with living no-fear Christianity. Before turning to the next chapter, take time to thank God for all the times he has been your shield and protected you, like he did in the car accident my dad and I experienced.

8

Therefore, Do Not Be Afraid

The Beinecke Rare Book and Manuscript Library is one of my favorite libraries in the world. Located on the campus of Yale University in New Haven, Connecticut, the library is an architectural wonder, complete with a six-story translucent veined marble and granite façade. During my PhD candidacy, I was part of the Visiting Scholars Program at Yale, and one day I found myself at the Beinecke Library. It was a delightfully sunny day, and the way in which the daylight filtered inside the central stacks was a sight to behold. With over one million rare books and manuscripts, there are literary treasures to behold as well, including the Jonathan Edwards Collection, complete with over one thousand of his sermon manuscripts, private theological notebooks, and personal correspondence.[1]

A Yale graduate, Edwards (1703–1758) is regarded as one of the finest American minds. His life as a pastor, theologian, revivalist preacher, and author was not only influential, it was varied.[2] As a young man, Edwards wrote an essay called "The Spider Letter" about flying spiders (he loved spiders!). He was also a key leader in the First Great Awakening,[3] served as a missionary to the Housatonic Indians of Massachusetts,[4] and was even dismissed from his longest-tenured pastorate because of disagreements related to the Lord's Supper. Edwards was surprisingly soft-spoken, certainly not worthy of the "fire and brimstone" reputation some have projected on him. He eventually became president of the College of New Jersey (Princeton University), but only a month into his tenure as president, he tragically died of a smallpox inoculation.

One of the most interesting discoveries about Edwards's life and ministry—something helpful for us yet today—is the subject of his first recorded sermon: Christian happiness. Amazingly, Edwards was only seventeen when he preached this sermon in late 1720. (Most articles claim Edwards was eighteen at the time, but after consulting church history professor and Edwards scholar Dr. Michael McMullen, who has published three volumes of previously unpublished Edwards's sermons, I am persuaded Edwards was seventeen, which is all the more astounding given the content.[5])

Edwards's sermon included three powerful points on Christian happiness based on Isaiah 3:10. (Timothy Keller's modernized version of Edwards's sermon is the basis of this section.)

1. **If you are a Christian, your bad things will turn out for good.** At the end of his first point, Edwards said, "Whatever the world does against you, you have this to comfort you, that Christ has overcome the world."

2. **Your good things can never be taken away from you.** Edwards said in this point, "How joyful and gladsome must the thoughts of Jesus Christ be to a Christian, to think how great a love Christ has for us, even to lay down his life and suffer the most bitter torments for our sake, who also now continually intercedes for us at the throne of grace; to consider that so great a person as the eternal Son of God, who also made the worlds, is his lord and master, and is not ashamed to call us brethren, who will come in and sup

with us, and us with him, and to see his arms expanded to embrace us and offering himself to be embraced by us."

3. **The best is yet to come.** Edwards concluded his sermon with a powerful thought reminiscent of Paul's words in 1 Corinthians 2:9: "And lastly, from the joyful hope and assured expectation of the enjoyment of the completion of happiness eternally hereafter, to pretend to describe the excellence, the greatness, or duration of the happiness of heaven, by the most artful composition of words, would be but to darken and cloud it."[6]

In many ways, this belief—that faith can dispel fear—launched Edwards's dynamic life and ministry, and it can launch you too. Here are more truths from that sermon:

You may look down upon all the whole army of worldly afflictions under your feet with a slight disregard . . . and consider with joy that, however great they are and however numerous, let them all join their forces together against you and put on their most rueful and dreadful habits, forms and appearances, and spend all their strength, vigor and violence with endeavors to do you any real hurt or mischief, and it is all in vain. You may triumph over them all knowing this: light afflictions, which are but for a moment, shall only work out for you a far more exceeding and eternal weight of glory.[7]

Yes, Christian happiness, anchored to the eternal truths of God's Word and character, dispels fear. In fact, it causes us to be bold in our witness for Jesus Christ because we are not ashamed or fearful.

Therefore, Do Not Be Afraid

In the Roman Empire of Paul's day, shame was to be avoided at all cost. To suffer defeat, to be imprisoned, to be punished, to be humiliated publicly, to be mocked, all were considered terribly shameful. The proclamation that the crucified Jesus of Nazareth was the Son of God and Savior of the world struck many in the Roman Empire as ludicrous because crucifixion was as shameful as it got. Great men—never mind a divine being—did not suffer crucifixion. Yet, the Christian Gospel proclaimed otherwise.

It is to the shame of crucifixion that Paul alludes when he boldly declares in his letter to the Christians of Rome, "I am not ashamed of the gospel: it is the power of God for salvation to every one who has faith" (Romans 1:16). Paul said this in the early years of his apostolic ministry, and he expressed it again near the end of his life when he wrote to Timothy, a pastor he had discipled: "Therefore I suffer as I do. But I am not ashamed, for I know whom I have believed, and I am sure that he is able to guard until that Day what has been entrusted to me" (2 Timothy 1:12).

Paul had met the risen Christ. It changed him and set his life on a whole new course. Paul had every confidence (note that he said, "I am sure") that God would keep and guard what had been entrusted to him. Paul is expressing the deep conviction that his faith and ministry were not in vain, not only in regard to himself but in regard to the very people to whom he had ministered. Jude, the brother of Jesus, expresses the same confidence in his letter, when he offers a concluding benediction: "Now to him who is able to keep you from falling and to present you without blemish before the presence of his glory with rejoicing" (Jude 24).

The disciples and apostles of Jesus could speak with such confidence because the risen Christ on several occasions had instructed them not to be afraid. In one of his early letters, Paul assures new believers that "the Lord is faithful; he will strengthen you and guard you from evil" (2 Thessalonians 3:3). Paul had visited Thessalonica during his second, tumultuous missionary journey (Acts 16–19) and was there scarcely one month before being driven away. He had stopped at Beroea, and though initially well received, he was again driven out of town (Acts 17:1–15). After a less than successful visit to Athens (Acts 17:16–33), Paul found himself in Corinth and, yet again, was fiercely opposed (Acts 18:1–6). Paul was dragged before the Roman proconsul Gallio, accused by fellow Jews of "persuading men to worship God contrary to the law" (Acts 18:13). Although the charges were dismissed, Paul did eventually depart for Ephesus (Acts 18:18–21).

What is interesting is that in the midst of all this conflict, the Lord appears to Paul in a vision and says, "Do not be afraid, but speak and do not be silent" (Acts 18:9). This word surely comforted Paul, because he stayed some time longer in Corinth. The result of this longer stay (in contrast to the brief stays at Thessalonica and Beroea) was the establishment of a large and thriving church at Corinth, whose strategic location (linking shipping to Asia Minor in the east and shipping to Italy in the west) greatly facilitated the growth of the church.

Much later in his ministry, when Paul was in custody in Caesarea Maritima, on the Mediterranean coast of Israel, an angel spoke to Paul and said, "Do not be afraid, Paul; you must stand before Caesar; and lo, God has granted you all those who sail with you" (Acts 27:24). As it turned out, the ship foundered in a violent storm and was wrecked on rocks near a beach on the island of Malta (Acts 27:9–44). However, having been encouraged by the word from heaven, Paul assured the Roman commander that all would make it to shore alive, and it was so (Acts 27:44). Paul eventually made it to Rome, under house arrest and awaiting trial before Caesar, where he had the opportunity to proclaim the gospel freely (Acts 28:14–31).

God's protective power was such that Paul used the imagery of armor, weapons, and battle in his writings. The apostle spoke of the shield, which, as we have noticed, appears often in Scripture, and he spoke of the sword, the breastplate, the helmet, and other military equipment. In his letter to the Christians of Ephesus (and elsewhere in Asia Minor), Paul draws on words and phrases from the prophecy of Isaiah, who says of the coming Messiah,

"Righteousness shall be the girdle of his waist, and faithfulness the girdle of his loins" (Isaiah 11:5) and of God himself, who came to the aid of Israel: "He put on righteousness as a breastplate, and a helmet of salvation upon his head; he put on garments of vengeance for clothing, and wrapped himself in fury as a mantle" (Isaiah 59:17).

Inspired by his own experience and by the prophetic words of Isaiah, Paul exhorts the believers of Ephesus:

> Finally, be strong in the Lord and in the strength of his might. Put on the whole armor of God, that you may be able to stand against the wiles of the devil. For we are not contending against flesh and blood, but against the principalities, against the powers, against the world rulers of this present darkness, against the spiritual hosts of wickedness in the heavenly places. Therefore take the whole armor of God, that you may be able to withstand in the evil day, and having done all, to stand. Stand therefore, having girded your loins with truth, and having put on the breastplate of righteousness, and having shod your feet with the equipment of the gospel of peace; besides all these, taking the shield of faith, with which you can quench all the flaming darts of the evil one. And take the helmet of salvation, and the sword of the Spirit, which is the word of God.
>
> Ephesians 6:10–17

I find it fascinating that Paul speaks of "having shod your feet with . . . the gospel of peace" (v. 15). Surely, he was alluding to the messenger of Isaiah 52:7, who announces "good tidings, who publishes peace," and who announces the reign of God. Paul also speaks of the "shield of faith" (v. 16). As noted at the beginning of the chapter 7, the first occurrence of the word *shield* (*māgēn*) is in Genesis 15:1, where God promised to protect Abraham. I think Paul has this very passage in mind, because it is in the same context, in Genesis 15:6, that we are told that Abraham "believed the LORD; and he reckoned it to him as righteousness." Abraham believed God, that is, he had *faith* in God, his *shield*. Genesis 15:6 was of huge importance for the apostle Paul and his conviction that justification before God came through faith not works (Galatians 2:16; 3:6; Romans 4:3). God promised Abraham that he would be a shield and protect him, and Abraham had faith that he would.

Paul never lost faith in his protective God. In prison, awaiting execution, Paul writes to Timothy and urges him to "rekindle the gift of God" that he possesses (2 Timothy 1:6). Literally, Paul is exhorting Timothy to bring the gift of God "back to life." He then assures the younger minister that "God did not give us a spirit of timidity but a spirit of power and love and self-control" (2 Timothy 1:7). Paul's reference to timidity may have been a deliberate allusion to the opening words of the book of Joshua, where God charges the successor of Moses: "Be strong and manly; do not be cowardly or frightened, for the Lord your God is with you in all places where you go" (Joshua 1:9, according to the Greek Old Testament). God will later repeat the charge to not fear, nor to be cowardly (see Joshua 8:1; cf. 10:8). Paul has used the noun equivalent of the verb that appears in the two passages from Joshua. In essence, Paul has exhorted Timothy not to be a coward. He must remember that God has given him "a spirit of power [*dynameōs*]" (2 Timothy 1:7). Possessing this power, Timothy can fulfill his mission and do the work of the ministry (cf. 2 Timothy 4:5).

One of the last writings to find its way into the New Testament is 1 John, a letter written by none other than the apostle John, one of the original disciples of Jesus. The main purpose of John's letter is to encourage the faithful to remain faithful, knowing that the risen Jesus is indeed the Messiah and that in him we have forgiveness of sin (1 John 1:9; 2:1). But the author of 1 John also knows that the little flock is under immense pressure by Roman society in general and by critics close at hand who insist that Jesus is not the Son of God and not the Messiah (1 John 2:22; cf. 2 John 7). The author of 1 John assures believers that they have nothing to fear, "because the one who is in you is greater than the one who is in the world" (1 John 4:4 NIV). Never forget that God, whose Spirit dwells within believers, is greater than the evil one, who dwells within the world.

As we have seen in the last two chapters, Israel's history, the ministries of Jesus and his apostles, and the words of Scripture provide ample evidence of God's protective presence, which, like a shield, a *māgēn*, protects us from the evil one and keeps us close to the Lord himself. Therefore, we should not be afraid. This is foundational for us as believers in Jesus Christ because we are constantly in a spiritual battle that requires capturing thoughts and making them obedient to Christ.

One of the main problems facing Christians is our expectations. We have somehow bought into the notion that following Jesus is a carefree sort of experience. This is false. As we have seen, following Christ assures us of God's peace, protection, and presence; however, we are immediately and constantly targeted by the flesh, the world, and the devil (1 John 2:16). The battle is won or lost in the mind, but we have weapons at our disposal that are mighty through God.

9

The Bible Weaponized and Misread

About half of us (48 percent) will experience mental illness at some point in our lifetime.[1] This represents an incredible ministry opportunity, where biblical precision will make an impact. Understanding Scripture better will help your perspective on your own mental and emotional health too. I say this because I have had numerous conversations with people in pain who have been hurt even more through misunderstandings or misstatements of Scripture. I also know others who have been hurt or confused by people misrepresenting God's character.

"Mental illness is not a personal or spiritual weakness. People with mental illness display the highest levels of courage, character and faith," says esteemed Christian psychiatrist Dr. Daniel Morehead. As we have touched on already, brain science is proving what psychiatrists and psychologists have been saying, namely, that mental illness is a physical disfunction of the brain. Mental illness is real. The great news is, the brain can heal, which should be another source of hope and reason that mental and physical health should get equal care. Dr. Morehead sheds encouraging light that "we are living in an exceptional time. . . . For the first time in human history we are now in a position as a society and the church to accept mental illness in a realistic and constructive way."[2]

When the relevant biblical teaching is understood properly—that is, in full context and in the light of what the original languages actually say—it should be clear that most cases of mental illness have nothing to do with sin, lack of faith, or even an evil spirit. It wasn't that long ago that many Christians—pastors and laity alike—told people who suffered with depression that their problem was due to sin or a lack of faith. Sadly, some people still think this. I have actually heard people say that all that was needed was more prayer and more Bible-reading or more effort in some way. The counsel was well intended, to be sure, but it was nonetheless very harmful and often only made the problem worse by adding a layer of guilt. Getting help for depression or mental illness is not an admission of moral failure or lack of spirituality, any more than going to a doctor to have a broken bone set is an admission of moral failure.

The tendency to "diagnose" mental problems as spiritual problems is likely closely tied to a dualistic worldview, in which the physical and the mental/spiritual are seen as two very separate realities. Under this worldview, we can accept that physical problems are not indicators of spiritual or mental health or of a lack of moral rectitude. But mental problems are seen as either spiritual or moral problems. Modern science, of course, has shown that the physical brain and the body's chemistry play a major role in mental health. Sometimes the brain breaks down or the body's chemistry is wrong. When that happens, there are problems. But these problems do not necessarily have any connection to spirituality or morality.

This is not to say that physical problems bear no relation to mental problems. Sometimes they do. Long-lasting illness and/or chronic pain can lead to depression. Sometimes disabilities and pain can be such that the sufferer wishes to die. There may be a spiritual problem here, but it is the result of a physical problem. Again, it is not the fault of the sufferer. Sometimes physical ailments not only bring on depression, they affect our thinking, creating a sense of worthlessness and desperation. Some maladies that are physical in nature can affect the brain and mind in such negative ways that it leads to suicide. Again, this is not the fault of the sufferer—and Christians should remember that. Offer to pray for those who suffer, but don't speak of their suffering as though through sin or lack of spirituality they have brought their suffering on themselves.

The Bible teaches that humans are physical/spiritual beings. These dimensions are not separated; they are unified. Christians believe that thanks to Christ's redemptive saving work, we will receive new bodies. We will be fully renewed in every way, physically and spiritually. We will not simply be spirits existing in heaven. This is the Good News we have in God's Son. Through his saving love, we can have redemption and restoration.

Unfortunately, some misunderstandings about mental illness in Christian circles stem from misunderstanding Scripture. I have listened to many sincere believers share how a passage of Scripture was weaponized (usually taken out of context) in a way that was, shall we say, anything but redemptive to the sufferer. The Bible is ancient literature from the Middle East. It is not modern literature from the West, which is how we moderns often read it. The failure to interpret Scripture in the light of its original context and meaning can lead to serious misinterpretation and misuse. Indeed, Scripture can be weaponized and employed in very harmful ways.

This is why Bible scholars must help the church in general—as well as help pastors, Sunday school teachers, and leaders in particular—with helpful interpretive tools so that we use the Scriptures in the timeless way they were intended and apply the truth of God's Word to healthy thinking and mental health. We do not want to commit biblical malpractice.

Have you ever *experienced* biblical malpractice? As I have written previously, the Bible has become a moving target in our day and age. One can strip it down, twist it, misread it, add to it, supplement it, and even overrule it, and, unfortunately, 95 percent of the typical congregation will not even realize it. Why? They do not know the Bible. Emblematic of the Bible's declining influence is a quote from Harper Lee's *To Kill a Mockingbird*. The character Miss Maudie says, "Sometimes the Bible in the hand of one man is worse than a whiskey bottle in the hand of [another]."

Most Christians know enough about the Bible to be dangerous.[3] One way the Scriptures have been confused and mismanaged stems from the phrase "a spirit of . . . [fill in the blank]." This has led some in the church historically down a terrible path of assigning blame for mental illness with the demonic world.

More than one hundred times in the Bible you will find the expression "spirit of" one thing or another. It is easy to assume that every occurrence of "spirit" is in reference to a sentient being, either the Holy Spirit providing assistance or comfort, or an evil spirit seeking to do us harm. People said to be afflicted with a "spirit of" something or other are thought to be possessed or under demonic influence. But are they? Is that what the Bible is talking about?

It is true, of course, that the Bible does indeed speak of the spirit world, the world of God's Spirit, as well as various dangerous spirits. But the word *spirit*, as we will see, sometimes has nothing to do with independent sentient beings.

Spirits and Emotions: Dangers from Without and from Within

In the fifth century BC, the Spirit of God moved the heart of the king of Persia to allow the Israelite captives to return home, to Jerusalem, to rebuild their city and their holy temple. They were eager to do so, but it was not easy. Few in number and limited in resources, they found themselves beset by enemies in their homeland. Work progressed slowly. It was discouraging. The work was in danger of stalling, so God raised up a prophet to exhort and encourage Israel. Zechariah, one of the very last prophets of the old era, said one of the most inspirational things you will find in the Old Testament. God gave Zechariah a prophetic word for Zerubbabel, the governor of the people of Israel: "This is the word of the LORD to Zerubbabel: 'Not by might, nor by power, but by my Spirit,' says the LORD of hosts" (Zechariah 4:6). The God of Abraham, the God of Moses, and the God of King David had spoken.

Through his prophet Zechariah, God had promised Zerubbabel that the task of rebuilding Jerusalem and her temple would be by the mighty power of God's Spirit, not by what human power that struggling Israel might be able to muster. If Zerubbabel were to rely on the strength of the manpower available to him, there would be no chance of success. But if he were to rely on the power of God's Spirit, there would be no chance of failure. Israel's human power might be limited, but God's power—what we might call divine pneumatic power—is unlimited.

There are other spirits, however, and they aren't always very helpful. The word "spirit," either in reference to the Spirit of God or in reference to other spirits, occurs in the Bible more than five hundred times. I have perused many of these passages and am amazed at the insights they offer. I want to share some of these insights with you in this chapter.

The Hebrew word for "spirit" is *ruaḥ*. The Greek word is *pneuma*, which is where we get the term *pneumatic*. The word can also mean "wind" or "breath." We find this meaning in the story of the creation of Adam: "The LORD God formed man of dust from the ground, and breathed into his nostrils the breath of life; and man became a living being" (Genesis 2:7). Although not stated, it was understood that what God "breathed" into man was his life-giving *Spirit*. Nowhere is the life-giving power of God's Spirit more in evidence than in Ezekiel's vision of the dry bones brought back to life. Through his prophet, God promises lifeless

Israel: "I will put my Spirit within you, and you shall live, and I will place you in your own land; then you shall know that I, the LORD, have spoken, and I have done it, says the LORD" (Ezekiel 37:14).

It is this association of spirit and wind that Jesus presupposes in his conversation with Nicodemus, a Jewish teacher keen to learn from Jesus. Here is part of that conversation:

> "Truly, truly, I say to you, unless one is born anew, he cannot see the kingdom of God." Nicodemus said to him, "How can a man be born when he is old? Can he enter a second time into his mother's womb and be born?" Jesus answered, "Truly, truly, I say to you, unless one is born of water and the Spirit, he cannot enter the kingdom of God. That which is born of the flesh is flesh, and that which is born of the Spirit is spirit. Do not marvel that I said to you, 'You must be born anew.' The wind blows where it wills, and you hear the sound of it, but you do not know whence it comes or whither it goes; so it is with every one who is born of the Spirit."
>
> John 3:3–8

To understand what Jesus is saying here, we need to understand what the Old Testament says about God's Spirit. The prophet Zechariah made it clear that God's Spirit—in contrast to human might (i.e., flesh)—is all-powerful. The prophet Ezekiel made it clear that God's Spirit gives life. That is why Jesus tells Nicodemus that he must be born of the Spirit. It is this new birth that admits one into the kingdom of God. This is why the apostle Paul urges believers to live by the Spirit (Romans 8:6–7).

However, often in Scripture, "spirit" refers to emotions, not a spiritual entity, as such. This point cannot be overstated! In a study that appeared on *Premier Christianity*'s website, David Instone-Brewer, a biblical scholar at Tyndale House in Cambridge, known for his expertise in early Judaism, reviews the Bible's use of "spirit" in reference to emotional and psychological disorders. It is important to understand these relevant passages, for they have a lot to say about mental and spiritual health. I gladly acknowledge my dependence on Instone-Brewer's well-written essay.[4]

In Exodus we are told that the Israelites, whom Moses wished to deliver from bondage in Egypt, initially refused to listen to Moses. They wouldn't listen, because, we are told, they, according to the Hebrew rendered literally, had "shortness [*qōtzer*] of spirit" (Exodus 6:9). By "shortness" one might think *impatience* (i.e., short-tempered) is meant, or perhaps *fatigue*, in the sense of having little endurance. But these are our meanings. Understood in accordance with ancient Semitic idioms, the meaning of *qōtzer* is "broken" or "discouraged." Hence, the RSV translates the passage: "they did not listen to Moses, because of their broken spirit and their cruel bondage." After years of bondage and hard toil, the people of Israel were beaten down, discouraged, demoralized. Moses' talk of deliverance seemed like little more than pie in the sky. The result is a "spirit of discouragement," or more literally, a "shortness of spirit."

We find another example of this use of "spirit" in the book of Joshua. After God divides the water of the Jordan River, allowing Israel to enter the Promised Land dry-shod, the Canaanites— Israel's enemies—were fearful. We are told that "their heart melted, and there was no longer any spirit in them" (Joshua 5:1). But the NIV translates it as "they no longer had the *courage* to face the Israelites" (emphasis mine), which captures the sense in a way that modern readers probably find easier to understand.

Most of us at one time or another experience deep, profound discouragement, perhaps a bit like the Canaanites, who no longer had any spirit in them. This is why in Scripture we are commanded to encourage one another: "Therefore encourage one another and build one another up . . . encourage the fainthearted, help the weak, be patient with them all" (1 Thessalonians 5:11, 14 ESV). Paul tells the Christians of Rome that he wishes to visit them, "that we may be mutually encouraged by each other's faith, both yours and mine" (Romans 1:12 ESV). He reminds the Romans of what had been written "in former days," that they will have hope "by the encouragement of the scriptures" (Romans 15:4). The apostle prays that "the God of steadfastness and encouragement" would make it possible for them to live in peace and harmony with one another (Romans 15:5). One hardly needs to be gifted to encourage someone, to lift them out of the funk of negative thinking and unhealthy self-criticism.

The Bible also speaks of a "spirit of jealousy" that could develop on the part of the husband of the wife (Numbers 5:14, 30). Both the King James and the RSV literally translate "spirit of jealousy," but there is no actual spirit, at least not in the sense of a being who acts. The Bible is referring to *emotion*, to *feelings*. This is why the NIV translates "feelings of jealousy." "Feelings" takes the place of "spirit." The NIV has paraphrased the text but has done so in a way, once again, that helps the modern reader.

Elsewhere in the Bible we are told that "God sent an evil spirit between Abimelech and the men of Shechem; and the men of Shechem dealt treacherously with Abimelech" (Judges 9:23 KJV, RSV). In the New Testament, "evil spirit" normally refers to a demon or "unclean spirit" that needs to be cast out. Such a spirit acts, speaks, and defies the work of God and Christ. But is that what is being talked about here in Judges 9? An evil entity? On the contrary, the Bible is talking about the emotions of anger or hatred. This is why the NIV translates it as "God stirred up animosity between" Abimelech and the men of Shechem. In fact, a little later in the story, a man named Gaal, son of Ebed, is identified as the cause of the hard feelings (Judges 9:26–31). It was indeed human behavior, not a literal evil spirit, that caused the animosity.

Probably the best known and least understood evil spirit in the Old Testament is the spirit that tormented King Saul. Several times we read that God sent an evil spirit against Saul (e.g., 1 Samuel 16:14–16, 23; 18:10; 19:9). In the first passage, we are told that "the Spirit of the LORD departed from Saul" (1 Samuel 16:14). The reference to "the Spirit of the LORD" could suggest that the "evil spirit" is, like the Holy Spirit, a sentient being. We are told that this evil spirit tormented Saul. The king's servants advise Saul: "Let our lord now command your servants, who are before you, to seek out a man who is skilful in playing the lyre; and when the evil spirit from God is upon you, he will play it, and you will be well" (1 Samuel 16:16). Sure enough, when David plays the lyre, the evil spirit leaves Saul (16:23). This evil spirit is so bad that even when David is playing the lyre, trying to soothe Saul, Saul tries to kill him (18:10–11; 19:9–10).

David is credited with 3,600 psalms—not just most of the psalms of the Old Testament's Psalter, but 364 songs to accompany daily burnt offerings, 52 Sabbath songs, and four songs "for charming the demon-possessed with music." The words "with music" clearly allude to the stories found in 1 Samuel, in which David plays the lyre and drives away the evil spirit that torments King Saul. Notwithstanding, most scholars do not think 1 Samuel is talking about a literal demon—a sentient evil spirit—but rather a mental disorder. They think this because the problem only overtakes Saul occasionally and David's music seems to calm him down. If Saul had been afflicted with an actual evil spirit, negative, harmful behavior would have been the norm. With this in mind, the ESV translates the phrase as "a harmful spirit." Perhaps it could be translated "a harmful emotion" or "spontaneous anger" (and I thank Dr. Instone-Brewer for these suggestions). King Saul may well have suffered from schizophrenia, which manifested itself from time to time as paranoia and perhaps also as depression. Because of this condition, he was convinced that David was plotting against him, seeking to take his throne, even though there was no evidence of any such thing. So on those occasions when his malady presented itself, Saul lashed out at David, not knowing that David was, in fact, loyal and trustworthy. The consequences of Saul's mental problems were tragic.

Jesus and the Spirits

Jesus encountered and cast out evil spirits that seem to have been sentient entities. On one occasion we are told that "there was in their synagogue a man with an unclean spirit" (Mark 1:23). Describing this spirit as "unclean" distinguishes the spirit from "Holy Spirit." That is, God's Spirit is holy, but the other spirits are evil or unclean. The spirit in the synagogue addressed Jesus, "What have you to do with us, Jesus of Nazareth? Have you come to destroy us? I know who you are, the Holy One of God" (Mark 1:24). The unclean spirit recognized Jesus and assumed that his purpose was the destruction of "us," that is, all evil spirits. But there is more. When the unclean spirit said, "I know who you are," he was threatening Jesus. Because he recognized Jesus and therefore knew his name, he could insert Jesus' name into a magic spell *against Jesus himself.* (We have a pretty good idea how this was understood in late antiquity because of the hundreds of exorcism texts that have been recovered.) But Jesus would have none of it. "Be silent, and come out of him!" Jesus commanded (Mark 1:25). The unclean spirit did, and the synagogue congregation was astounded, saying, "What is this? A new teaching! With authority he commands even the unclean spirits, and they obey him" (Mark 1:27).

On another occasion, Jesus encountered a far more dangerous case of possession. On the eastern side of the Sea of Galilee, in an area mostly populated by Gentiles, Jesus is met by "a man with an unclean spirit, who lived among the tombs," whom "no one could bind" (Mark 5:2–3). This man could break the chains and fetters with which he had been bound, even as Samson of old could do (Judges 16:12). Worse still, the demonized man identified himself as "Legion; for we are many" (Mark 5:9). Nothing could be more frightening for people in late antiquity than to encounter a deranged man with superhuman strength, possessed by a legion of unclean spirits. I should mention, too, that the name "Legion" would have conjured up in the minds of everyone the mighty Roman legions that dominated the Mediterranean world, including Israel. Yet, when this so-called Legion met Jesus, it surrendered and begged for terms (Mark 5:10–11). It is no wonder that Jesus' fame as healer and exorcist spread across the land (Mark 1:28; 6:56).

But not everyone with mental and spiritual problems was possessed with evil spirits. An important example of this is seen in a passage in Matthew. In reference to Jesus' growing fame, the evangelist says, "So his fame spread throughout all Syria, and they brought him all the sick, those afflicted with various diseases and pains, demoniacs, epileptics, and paralytics, and he healed them" (Matthew 4:24). The word translated "demoniacs" is *daimonizomenous*. It could also be translated "demonized." It is the same word from which we get "demon." The word translated "epileptics" in Matthew 4:24 is *selēniazomenous*. It literally means "moon-struck" (from whose Latin equivalent we get the word *lunatic*) and probably should be translated "insane" or "mentally ill." The two words, *demonized* and *mentally ill*, are found side by side, as though describing two conditions. They may overlap, but they are not the same. The point that is implied is that not all people who suffer from mental problems are possessed. Some simply suffer from mental problems, and Jesus knew the difference. We must prayerfully represent and emulate Jesus by knowing the difference too (which is why the assistance of biblically based counselors and therapists is so important for pastors and the church today). David Instone-Brewer offers a refreshing point:

> Jesus knew that people can have mental illnesses just as they have other illnesses. *And* he knew that people can be troubled by demons. If we don't recognize this too, we can increase the suffering of those with psychological or psychiatric problems by falsely diagnosing demonic activity. Through prayer, demonic troubles can generally be addressed fairly quickly. However, illnesses of the mind can take much longer to heal, and often recur. God can wonderfully heal these maladies, like others, but many people have to live with them. Just as society is now more open about mental health than

ever before, the Church, too, can shake off the unhelpful attitudes of the past by offering acceptance and practical support, and by bringing those who are suffering before God in prayer.[5]

Sometimes mental illness and demon possession go hand in hand, the former opening up the possibility of the latter, or the latter causing the former. We may have an example of this in the case of boy and his distraught father (see Matthew 17:14–20; Mark 9:14–27; Luke 9:37–43). The father tells Jesus, "Teacher, I brought my son to you, for he has a dumb spirit; and wherever it seizes him, it dashes him down; and he foams and grinds his teeth" (Mark 9:17–18). Should the reference to a "dumb" or "mute spirit" be understood as a sentient being? Or is it a condition? In Matthew's account (17:15), a Greek word that means "moon-struck" is used. But at the end of the story, Matthew (like Mark) says Jesus spoke and the "demon" came out of the boy. Luke says Jesus "rebuked the unclean spirit" (Luke 9:42). In the case of the tormented boy, we do not know which happened first—the demon or the illness—but Jesus drove out the one and healed the other. (In all three gospel accounts the evil spirit is driven out, then the boy is healed.)

But let me return to the story of the man on the east side of the Sea of Galilee, who had been possessed of a legion of evil spirits. When the frightened pig herders returned with people from the nearby town, they saw the man "sitting there, clothed and in his right mind" (Mark 5:15). The Greek word translated "right mind" is *sōphrounta*, which means of sound thinking or mind. The word is sometimes used in contexts of modesty and decorum, which applies in the present case. After all, we are told that after Jesus had healed him, he was "clothed." The implication was that prior to his encounter with Jesus, he was dressed in rags or was perhaps naked. The parallel passage in Luke, in fact, explicitly states that the man "for a long time . . . had worn no clothes" (Luke 8:27).

This story reminds us that mental illness can often affect our sense of dignity and self-esteem. The man Jesus encountered was a mental and emotional wreck. After his encounter with Jesus, he was transformed. He sat before Jesus, clothed, focused, and able to speak rationally. The man now had a story to tell and Jesus encouraged him to tell it: "Go home to your friends, and tell them how much the Lord has done for you, and how he has had mercy on you" (Mark 5:19). And he did so, proclaiming throughout the region "how much Jesus had done for him," and everyone was amazed (5:20).

The Healing Process

It is important to mention that a healing might take place in a moment, but recovery from mental illness often takes much longer. The Gospels record a selection of Jesus' mighty deeds. They are impressive, and they are probably the best examples. Although miracles still happen today—and Craig Keener's impressive two-volume work, *Miracles* (Baker Academic, 2011), provides several well-documented reports—most physical and mental healing occur as a process, sometimes over a long period.

I want to emphasize that mental illness is not usually the result of moral or spiritual failure. Nor is it always the result of evil, as we have seen. It is true that mental illness can be the result of negative habits and foolish, destructive behavior. More importantly, whatever mental challenge one faces, there is a treatment plan. According to Dr. Matthew Stanford (and I cannot over-recommend his organization, The Hope and Healing Center and Institute), "Research has consistently shown that clergy, not psychologists or other mental health professionals, are the most common sources of help sought in times of psychological distress."[6]

There is still a stigma around mental illness, but it wasn't too long ago that it caused such shame that families sent loved ones with mental illness to institutions, sometimes called asylums. There these poor sufferers remained, in some cases for the rest of their lives. So embarrassing was mental illness people often refused even to acknowledge the existence of family members with the problem.

One case that caught my attention a few years ago concerned Lord Randolph Churchill (1849–1895), the father of Winston Churchill, who went on to become Great Britain's greatest prime minister. Lord Randolph suffered from mental illness, which his family tried to hide, or explain as temperament or eccentric behavior. In fact, Lord Randolph was seriously ill and, so far as we know, never received proper treatment. He died at a relatively young age (a month short of forty-six), never reaching the greatness he might have achieved. Even Winston himself was plagued with depression, which he euphemistically called his "black dog."

I am encouraged that today, more and more churches recognize that good people can and do suffer from mental illness, and even addiction, much as people suffer from physical ailments. Mental illness should not be a cause of shame, any more than physical illness should be a cause of shame. Modern medicine, counseling, and prayer go hand in hand in bringing about healing, whether physical or mental. Dr. Morehead is, again, helpful:

> It should be clear that mental illness is not caused by sin or a lack of faith, and neither is it cured by repentance or increased faith. In the past, some people have been told that they are depressed because they lack faith, or that they don't need mental health treatment, just to practice their faith. We now know that this is wrong, just as wrong as telling someone with a broken leg that they just need faith, and that they should not go to the doctor to get the leg treated.[7]

With better biblical precision, rather than weaponizing or misreading Scripture we can compassionately be part of the healing equation. The importance of our faith in this healing equation cannot be overemphasized; therefore, we need to make sure we are always representing the spirit of Jesus (compassion) and accurately applying the truths of the Scriptures (interpretation) to every affliction. This is the gospel in action.

10

Holistic Happiness:
Mind, Body, and Soul

An Interview with Rick Tague, MD, MPH

There is a direct and strong correlation between our physical fitness and our mental fitness (our mental peace). Dr. Rick Tague (MD, MPH, and TM)[1] has served well over twenty thousand patients through his Center for Nutrition and Preventive Medicine clinics in Kansas City and Topeka, Kansas. Dr. Tague is board certified with the American Board of Obesity Medicine and the American Board of Family Medicine. He graduated from Tulane Medical School with degrees in medicine and public health. He is a member of Alpha Omega Alpha Medical Honor Society. Most importantly, Dr. Tague has been serving patients in the pursuit of optimum health since 1996, focusing on nutrition and weight management, along with a healthy lifestyle, as key strategies.

I am one of Dr. Tague's twenty thousand patients, and I have been blessed by his care since 2009. There is no way I could have the physical energy, personal wellness, and mental peace to serve my family of seven and also fulfill the calling of God on my life without Dr. Tague's influence, education, and ministry in my life. This book is about experiencing God's peace in every area of our lives; therefore, it is pertinent at this point to understand how important our physical life is to our mental and spiritual life, and for this I have asked Dr. Tague questions directly relating to our physical health and mental peace. If our nutrition is optimal and we are trim and fit, our brain thinks better, our mood is better, and we're happier, more productive people. I asked Dr. Tague six questions related to optimum health because I am fascinated by the integration of physical health, soul-care, and mental health.[2] As we will see, there is much to learn and apply.

1. Our Goal Is Optimum Health: Disease Prevention and Healthy Brain Function Are Key Outcomes

Dr. Tague, will you describe your nearly forty years of experience in family medicine, preventive medicine, nutrition, weight management, and obesity medicine? You're a metabolism (body chemistry) expert. You're board certified and oversee busy medical clinics. Give us a background of your practice and expertise.

Dr. Tague: The foundation for my medical practice developed while at Kansas State University, studying for a career in chemical engineering. Entering my final year of school, God directed me into medicine. Little did I know that my education in chemical engineering would eventually be applied to the metabolism and biochemistry of my patients, helping them achieve optimum health and the goals of being trim, fit, healthy, and happy.

After Kansas State, I enrolled at Tulane University School of Medicine as well as Tulane's School of Public Health. That simultaneous training was transformational. During the daytime

I would go to medical school, where we would generally learn how to diagnose diseases and then develop treatment plans involving prescription medications and/or a procedure. Although not ideal, that's basically still how medical schools operate—they train physicians to make a diagnosis and write a prescription or do a procedure.

However, in the evenings, after medical school classes, I would go across the street and study at the public health school, learning about nutrition and disease prevention. There we were trained repeatedly that "No, it's not about diagnosing disease; it's about preventing disease." Anytime you can prevent disease, it's far wiser and more valuable to the individual and to the population as a whole than waiting until a disease is present and trying to treat it. This multifaceted educational context gave me a framework of thought regarding my future medical career. I decided that from day one of my medical practice, **I would be committed to using the power of preventive medicine strategies with my patients.**

One of my favorite textbooks, *Clinical Preventive Medicine*, gave me clarity. Every chapter related to current epidemic diseases came down to two conclusions: One, we need to control our weight and not become overweight or obese; and two, excellent nutrition is critical to experience optimum health. Heart disease, stroke, type 2 diabetes, high blood pressure, osteoarthritis, cancers—essentially all the diseases that are epidemic in our nation right now—can typically be prevented through weight control and excellent nutrition.

When I started my practice, I immediately implemented these principles and used nutrition and weight loss when appropriate with my patients, and found it was far more powerful than prescriptions for achieving health. People were happier with the results, and they ended up closer to optimum health, which really should be the goal for each of us, especially as believers being good stewards of our bodies.

2. God Made Us in His Image. More than Body, We Are Also Soul and Spirit

Genesis 2:7 is a key passage: "Then the LORD God formed man of dust from the ground, and breathed into his nostrils the breath of life; and man became a living being." Dr. Tague, what I have learned from you in the years that I've been one of your patients is that each of us is an integrated whole, and when we take action in one dimension of our life, it impacts all other dimensions or parts of our life. From your perspective as a Christian medical doctor, what is holistic health, and how does it relate to God creating man as the trichotomy of body, soul, and spirit?

Dr. Tague: I share a handout with my patients that has a diagram of body, soul, and spirit, because I believe it's impossible to experience optimum health without addressing both tangible (the body) and intangible (soul and spirit) aspects of life. An example is someone who is experiencing chronic stress (lack of peace), and they come to me with depression and high blood pressure. Even if I prescribe an antidepressant and blood pressure medication, it would not translate to peace, which is in the spiritual domain of life and a fruit of the Holy Spirit. If I were unable to address that intangible side of life—perhaps spiritual or relational distress—it would be impossible to help him or her achieve optimum health. You see, spiritual health, including peace, is a key to true optimum health. If someone needs peace, no medical prescription will provide it. The only real solution, I believe, is to turn to God, the ultimate and only true source of peace. When appropriate, I ask patients how they are doing spiritually. I may then encourage them to meditate on verses related to peace for battling fears, anxieties, worries, and uncertainties. When God's truth transforms our thoughts and the Spirit of God touches our hearts and souls, a supernatural peace is possible, one which neither the world nor prescriptions can offer.

Experiencing God's Shalom through
Scripture Memorization

It is possible to change our focus from stress issues to God's peace. "I go through certain Bible verses in my mind when worry starts to overwhelm me," says Dr. Tague. For years he has recommended that patients memorize the following verses because stressful thoughts can sneak up at any moment: Psalm 119:23, Psalm 119:51, Proverbs 14:30, Proverbs 22:10, Isaiah 26:3, Isaiah 41:10, Matthew 6:33–34, Matthew 11:28–29, Luke 3:14, John 14:27, Romans 12:18, Romans 16:17, Philippians 4:6–7, and Proverbs 18:9.

Think about the world. What it gives so often is fear, insecurity, and a damaged self-esteem, often related to criticisms and our worries about what people think or say. This is the opposite of what God wants for us.

God values us and builds our self-esteem. He calls us his children. He calls us forgiven. Through the Holy Spirit, he provides joy and peace. He is constantly transforming us to be more and more like Christ. The hope he gives is opposite of what the world and our spiritual enemy, the devil, gives. And, unfortunately, it is also opposite of what people may offer us.

3. Our Bodies Are the Temple of the Holy Spirit

Dr. Tague, the Bible offers us clues about physical, mental, and spiritual health. From a medical perspective, what does 1 Corinthians 6:19 mean to you—"Do you not know that your body is a temple of the Holy Spirit within you, which you have from God? You are not your own"?

Dr. Tague: Let me start by sharing a personal example that is also backed up by research. We all have physical shortcomings that are a result of the fall (see Genesis 3). Adam and Eve were born with perfect physical health, but everyone since that time has had some shortcomings and a tendency toward a lack of health in some areas. For many, including myself, it is a challenge to maintain a healthy and joyful mood. I've found that although my spiritual health may be excellent, I may still suffer from feelings of discouragement or distress or I may not be as hopeful and positive as I should be. Rather than being a spiritual issue, it can be as simple as a deficiency of certain "feel good" chemicals in my brain. As humans, we feel better when we have more of those healthy brain messenger compounds, including endorphins, serotonin, and dopamine.

I am analytical regarding my mood. I've observed that when I spend time with the Lord in the morning—asking for his joy and peace and to be filled with his Spirit, confessing any wrongdoing or impurities in my heart and mind—I experience more joy. But I also know that when I run in the morning for twenty minutes or so, my mood is remarkably better at the end of my run than before it. On days when I only have my devotional time without my run, my mood may be okay but not at my potential for optimum mental health, productivity, and ministry to others. On days when I run, my mood is simply better. It's easier to experience joy and peace. I have more spiritual energy. I am more loving to people, more patient, and more kind. I feel happier. I am more visionary and more productive at work. It seems peculiar: Can't prayer be enough to feel great?

After researching the science, I now understand that running in the morning rejuvenates the healthy, "feel good" brain chemicals, including endorphins, serotonin, and dopamine—biochemical compounds that energize our minds. Stress, disrupted sleep, and poor nutrition do the opposite and rob us of those healthy brain chemicals. There's no question that time with the Lord, worshiping him and confessing and repenting of sins, helps to reset our brain chemistry. Much research has shown that those practicing their faith are less depressed and healthier. But, for me, my morning twenty minutes of moderately intense fitness time, becoming sweaty and short of breath, with the physical impact of jogging, elevates my mood and productivity for the day. You see, our bodies, including our brains, are part of who we are, just as the Holy Spirit is part of who we are. It's a whole package: body, soul, and spirit. To be at our best, we need to invest time and energy pursuing our best possible health spiritually, physically, and emotionally. I work at it daily, so should we all.

One study looked at two groups of depressed individuals. One group was given a common antidepressant and the other group was asked to spend thirty minutes on a treadmill three times a week. Researchers then methodically measured the individuals' moods using a standardized scale and found that those on the treadmill experienced better moods and more improvement from their depression than those using medication alone.

Another key to a healthy mood is proper nutrition. You see, essential nutrients, like vitamins and minerals, are necessary for creating healthy brain chemistry. If we are suffering from a nutrient deficiency, our brain and body function will suffer. Good nutrition helps our brains think better, improves our mood, and also helps us be more productive. Sadly, malnutrition, in the form of essential nutrient deficiencies, has become an epidemic across our nation. "Over" nutrition of empty calories contributes to people being overweight. But we often suffer from "under" nutrition—not getting enough essential vitamins, minerals, and essential fatty acids. A key example is magnesium, which is deficient in the diets of 85 percent of Americans. The challenge is, it is almost impossible to get enough magnesium in our foods, and low magnesium is associated with depression. In fact, one study involved individuals who did not respond to common antidepressants. When they took magnesium supplements in therapeutic amounts, the depression resolved in a significant majority of those individuals.

Multiple studies have shown that magnesium can be a great aid for depression and anxiety symptoms. The brain simply does not function well when it's short of nutrients. Other important nutrients for brain and mental health include omega 3 fatty acids, vitamin B6, folate, vitamin C, and iron. Indeed, we need the whole spectrum of vitamins and minerals for the brain to function normally. And if the brain is not functioning normally, it's hard to feel our best and experience all the joy that God has for us.

4. Is Optimum Health the Same for Everyone?

Dr. Tague, optimum health is clearly an emphasis in your practice. As a Christian medical doctor, what does that mean as you work with each of your patients?

Dr. Tague: *Optimum*, of course, means "the ultimate, the preferred, the best possible outcome." *Health* includes the concept of wellness, but it's the lack of disease, the lack of pain, the lack of stress, the lack of unnecessary suffering or other psychological or physical disturbances that people experience.

There are limitations when it comes to optimum health. For example, if a person is in a car accident and becomes paralyzed from the waist down, optimum health will mean something different for that individual than it would for someone else. What we're looking for is the best possible outcome for an individual in their particular physical body. Our body can be likened to a house or tent that we live in—and each "tent" has its limitations. We all have certain limitations, so optimum health goals need to be individualized, so the goals are achievable for the individual. For example, if a person has a chronic, incurable disease, he or she can still achieve *their* optimum health.

It still means taking care of the body in every possible way, including stress management, sleep, nutrition, etc. I refer to stress as the "health terminator"! It's deadly. And God designed us to require sleep. Sleep is mandatory for health; we are rejuvenated by sleep. Psalm 127:2 tells us that God blesses his beloved even while they sleep, so getting that seven to seven and a half hours of sleep is important for everyone. As discussed earlier, getting proper nutrition is mandatory for optimum health; otherwise there will be deficiencies that will hold us back from experiencing best health outcomes. An example would be certain vitamin deficiencies, such as folate or vitamin C, that may increase the risk of cancer.

Another important aspect of optimum health is weight control. Most of our bodies are not meant to carry more than thirty pounds or so of body fat. We need some fat, but once we gain an excess, the expanding fat tissue can't maintain an adequate blood supply and the tissues start to break down. Then the white blood cells have to go and clean up the situation of those dying cells, which creates inflammation, which is why overweight people have a chronic state of inflammation. That's not optimum health. Those inflammatory proteins can cause joint disease, aches, fatigue, and a general lack of well-being. Being overweight also increases the risk of diabetes, heart disease, cancer, and stroke.

There are diseases that are inevitable, in part because we live in these frail human bodies. Disease will happen. Death is inevitable. Our bodies are failing. Still, being a good steward of our bodies is the right thing to do and gives us the best chance for optimum health on this journey through life.

5. Immediate Steps to Care for Your Body and Mind

Dr. Tague, what are the steps for caring for the body and the mind? What are the most important immediate steps?

Dr. Tague: There are five keys. First, get enough sleep. Sleep disturbance has a strong association with increased risk of diabetes and cancer and high blood pressure, heart disease, and stroke.

Research says seven to seven and a half hours of sleep is optimal for the vast majority of individuals.

Second, have daily fitness time. A study done by the Cooper Clinic in Dallas showed that people getting an average **nine minutes of daily fitness time** (exertion to the point of becoming sweaty and short of breath), live, on average, 6.2 years longer. That's investing an hour a week. I generally run twenty minutes every day, which is two miles, but if I don't have time for that, I make sure I get my nine of fitness time every day. Most of us can achieve this simple goal with a little planning.

Third, work daily on stress management. I have a saying: *I move stress in to my past and out of my future.* Here's what I mean: We often bring stress on ourselves through unwise decisions or unhealthy relationships, or being around unhealthy people and making bad decisions that have bad outcomes. The thing is, God promises wisdom to all who ask him. James 1:5 says, "If any of you lacks wisdom, you should ask God, who gives generously to all without finding fault, and it will be given to you" (NIV).

Wisdom involves making right decisions, and when it comes to stress, making right decisions can push stress out of your present, out of your future, and into your past. Sometimes this involves making peace with someone, so if I've offended an individual or they have offended me, the Bible instructs us very clearly to go and talk to that individual in order to resolve the situation. If the person is unreasonable and not open to being peaceable, it may mean deciding to create a boundary between yourself and that person so you can protect yourself from that stress.

Do what you can to resolve stress in your life. Get wisdom from God through his Word. Let the Holy Spirit guide your thoughts and your mind to solutions, and then seek counsel and help from wise people God has put in your life.

Fourth, be intentional about what you put into your body. Our bodies are "wonderfully made" by God (Psalm 139:14 NIV). Don't they deserve wonderful nutrition? Daily fruit, vegetables, nuts, lean sources of protein, healthy oils are examples. There's no way to have a healthy body without healthy nutrients being put into our physical body. We need to eat well, stay well hydrated with water and other healthy beverages, and, I believe, take proper nutritional supplements to achieve optimal intake of essential nutrients.

Finally, maintain a healthy weight. Being significantly overweight is a disease of the fat cells, but it can often sabotage health of the entire body. Even losing 5 to 10 percent of your body weight can be transformational to health. Get medical help if you're struggling with your weight.

6. Transformation Begins in Our Soul

I often say, "Hope comes when we have a plan." After caring for more than twenty thousand patients, what is your number-one recommendation for achieving optimum health in body, soul, and spirit?

Dr. Tague: Transformation has to begin in our soul—the soul being our mind, our will, and our emotions. The mind houses our thoughts, and our thoughts are often driven by input from outside sources. So, by getting thoughts into our mind that are wise and health promoting, it gives us the opportunity then to make right decisions, and that's where the "will" comes in.

I describe our will as a switch that says *I will*, or *I won't*. In everyday life, we're confronted with all sorts of decisions. If we don't have the proper knowledge base, we can't make proper decisions. But once we're aware of an issue, such as getting proper rest, we have the knowledge to decide, *I will get proper rest*, or *I won't*. Those who use their will to make healthy decisions are saying to themselves, *I need to move stress into my past and out of my future*. They use their will to make the right decision, even if it's difficult, to bring about a desired outcome.

Most people, unfortunately, are not making the right daily decisions to achieve optimum health. Unfortunately, many lack proper knowledge, but for others, they know what's right but they're not using their will to make the right decision. They're deciding not to consume fruits and vegetables on a regular basis, for example, and are missing out on experiencing their optimum level of health and vitality and mental function and mood. In all areas of our life, we need to seek knowledge and ask God for his wisdom to direct our thoughts and actions. He wants the best for us. Let's cooperate with him!

Let's Save Lives

Compassion, Prevention, and Intervention

As a Bible scholar, I never thought I would be ministering so extensively by answering questions related to mental illness and suicide. As an apologist, I am called to help answer the questions of today with unchanging biblical truth. Little did I know people would have so many questions related to anxiety, suicide, and associated mental illnesses. I have discussed these issues extensively in Bible studies, books, magazine articles, newspaper essays, and various blogs, media programs, and shows.[1] This chapter is dependent on much of my prior work in publishing, but not only the written work. In major cities and small towns, both in America and the United Kingdom, I have heard from so many tragically affected by suicide. I have stood with them. I have prayed with them. Often I have wept with them. I have heard many heart-wrenching stories.

This chapter is dedicated to helping you make the next most important step for yourself and others.

It's vital to know that there is hope. You are not alone.

Unlike many illnesses and diseases that are readily discernible, depression, anxiety, and other mental health issues are often invisible to the naked eye, yet their effects can be devastating. Despite the prevalence of mental health issues, churches often neglect to address these problems. I've called this widespread phenomenon "the church of invisible diseases."[2] The church is no stranger to suffering, but when it comes to mental health issues, there is silence from most pulpits. As Christians, though, we have a responsibility to step up and bring awareness and help for those suffering from the invisible disease. My hope is this chapter will help answer questions about the church's role in the fight against depression and suicide.

I have received many messages after addressing the subject of mental illness from a biblical worldview. Holly emailed me the following, which I think is a helpful example of what happens when we break the silence in our church services:

Hello Jeremiah—

I just wanted to thank you again for all you said this morning about mental illness and suicide. As a licensed professional counselor, I have the same discussion with clients all the time. Somehow, it's often not enough coming from me. I'm either "getting paid to say that" or I was taught to say it by some psychology school. It means so much more coming from the pulpit. Pastors should say EXACTLY what you said from EVERY pulpit in EVERY church on a regular basis. I can only imagine the number of lives you touched just this morning. Thank you!

Suicide is a national public health crisis, but suicides are preventable. Here's how you can save lives right now.

Mother Teresa once remarked, "If I look at the masses, I will never act." Unfortunately, many have a detached view of the grim influence of what is now a public health crisis: mental illness. One in four people lives with a mental health condition, which means someone you know has likely had thoughts of suicide. Mental illness touches us all. The World Health Organization makes it clear that suicide is a public health crisis.[3] Suicide has reached epidemic levels. Yet suicide is preventable. Unfortunately, most people do not know where to start, feeling unprepared and ill equipped to save lives. As I have written throughout this book, I've been asked thousands of questions through my work at Christian Thinkers Society. It may surprise you to learn that the most common questions are about suicide and mental illness.

After hearing me speak on the subject of suicide, a veteran police officer made a profound observation: "Officers must stop treating mentally ill people exclusively as suspects, and instead treat them as hurting people." Unfortunately, these days, people experiencing psychological distress often wind up in one of two places: jail or the emergency room.

All of us are an essential factor in the healing equation. We must initiate lifesaving dialogue. Here's a plan of compassion, prevention, and intervention:

1. **The church must be more accepting of people's pain.**
   Mental illness does not separate people from the love of God, and it shouldn't separate us from the love of our church, either. After speaking at a dynamic church near Miami, Florida, with over eighty nationalities represented among the church's diverse congregation, I received the following email from a neuropsychologist:

   > *Dear Mr. Johnston:*
   > *I attended the service this Saturday at Oasis Church. It was great that you were able to touch on various important subjects that are affecting Christianity, persistence in the faith, as well as coming to Christ in the community. I work as a neuropsychologist, and in my*

line of work I primarily work with individuals that are experiencing life-changing events that naturally make them question God's love and even His existence. Typically, they come to me during their recovery process. Interestingly I am also receiving church leaders that are enduring significant losses and their faith is being shaken.

One of the difficulties I am encountering is that churches are not very loving and accepting of their pain. It is very challenging for me to educate others in different churches as their approach tends to be a lovingly harsh one. The church body needs to be greatly educated to embrace with loving-kindness when the body comes to them brutally injured. In fact, over 90% of Christians that I have received in my office have expressed suicidal ideations and how they feel that the church body only reminds them of their limited faith.

I just wanted to share I am glad that you are providing education to others, as I am confronted with these issues frequently.

It is important to note we should not celebrate or glorify pain, but we should acknowledge it. The church is a spiritual hospital, not a museum for perfect people. As I have said, the church has generally avoided conversations at the intersection of faith, suicide, and mental illness. It is time to ask ourselves, what would Jesus Christ want us to do? I believe he would initiate a lifesaving dialogue and there would be no issue unaddressed.

2. **The church must stop the stigma, shame, and exclusion.** Start the conversation. Remove the stigma. Stop the isolation. Each September in the United States is suicide prevention month; September 8–14 is National Suicide

Prevention Week; and September 10 is World Suicide Prevention Day.

Even so, too many feel the sharp edge of stigma projected on "the suicidal type." They feel they are to blame for their mental illness, and do not seek help. Stigma leads to shame, shame leads to isolation, and isolation is the last stop on the brutal path to suicide. No one should ever have to suffer in silence. No one is unaffected by mental illness. If you have not personally struggled with mental illness, chances are that your friend, spouse, child, co-worker, or neighbor has. As Christians, we need to build awareness of the problem and remove the stigma, because mental illness is widespread and affects everyone. The ministry of Jesus focused on removing barriers to belief and restoring people who were suffering. The church needs to follow Jesus' example. Yet a Lifeway Research survey found that 66 percent of pastors rarely or never address the subject of mental illness from their pulpits. The same survey revealed that the majority of churchgoers wish their pastors would talk about it.[4]

I have asked this question in other writings, but when you read the words *mental illness*, what pictures or words come to your mind?[5] Many stigmatize the mentally ill as people in hospital gowns, committed deep inside a psych ward. But that is a very inaccurate depiction of someone with a mental illness. Would it surprise you to learn that people with mental illnesses worship at your church and probably attend your Bible study group with you? It is very sad that we say so little about mental illness in the church. We act as if it does not exist. Rarely do we hear sermons or read Bible study materials on this topic. It has left some Christian leaders in a quandary because in almost every family, at least one person is suffering from mental illness. One article summarized the findings of the Lifeway Research study and further added that "nearly 1 in 4 pastors (23 percent) acknowledge they have 'personally struggled with mental illness,' and half of those pastors said the illness had been diagnosed, according to the poll."[6]

One positive development I have noticed in the last five years is the fact that some churches have organized community events on the subject of mental health. I know because I have spoken at several of these events. These churches are leading the way in their communities by involving not only biblical counselors and church staff, but also inviting local law enforcement, school leadership, university professors, local mental health support groups, and even civil and political leaders to participate. Kay Warren and I spoke at a conference in Alabama appropriately titled "Not Alone," which also featured Attorney General Steve Marshall, who had recently lost his wife to suicide. The event was Christ-honoring and filled with hope. So please know that there are some phenomenal templates of how churches are using faith-inspired events to have these important conversations!

3. **Know the facts and fallacies of suicide.** More U.S. citizens kill themselves than kill one another each year, stark evidence proving we are all far more dangerous to ourselves than we are to other people. Until you have been brought to the brink, you may not understand the intensity of another individual's struggle that might trigger a suicide attempt. Invisible illnesses of the brain have the power to isolate you, cause you to cease to be a productive member of society, shorten your lifespan, and even kill you.

Respond to each statement below:

True or False: Talking about suicide will plant the idea in a depressed person's mind.

True or False: People who talk about suicide usually do not follow through with it.

True or False: Most suicides occur without warning.

True or False: When depression lifts, suicide is no longer a concern.

True or False: A suicidal person cannot be talked out of it if he or she is intent on dying.

True or False: Only certain people are the suicidal type.

True or False: African American men complete suicide at the same rates as Caucasian men.

True or False: Only insane or "crazy" people complete suicide.

True or False: Women threaten suicide, but only men complete suicide.

True or False: If a person has survived a suicide attempt, the likelihood of a second attempt is diminished.

True or False: People who complete suicide usually have not sought medical help prior to the attempt.

True or False: Suicide is a new phenomenon. No one in the Bible attempted or completed suicide.

All of these statements are false, and yet many of them are common fallacies.[7]

Fact: Can a Christian commit suicide? Yes, Christians, including pastors, do commit suicide. As we will discuss, though, suicide should not be considered an "unpardonable sin." Still, respected doctors and authors Frank Minirth and Paul Meier make an important point: "Suicide is a sin just as murder is a sin. 'Thou shalt not kill' (Exodus 20:13) applies to our own lives as well as the lives of others. Suicide is never God's will!"[8] There are six suicides in the Old Testament Scriptures and one suicide in the New Testament (all men). Drs. Minirth and Meier make the point clear: "None of the men who committed suicide was at that time acting in accordance with the will of God."[9]

There is no question, for a believer to die by suicide is a poor testimony, regardless of the situation. God is the author of life, and only he should bring a life to its conclusion. He desires us to follow him, and he will bless us with purpose and lasting fulfillment. God heals the brokenhearted and binds up their wounds (Psalm 147:3).

> Today I have given you the choice between life and death, between blessings and curses. Now I call on heaven and earth to witness the choice you make. Oh, that you would choose life, so that you and your descendants might live! You can make this choice by loving the LORD your God, obeying him, and committing yourself firmly to him. This is the key to your life.
>
> Deuteronomy 30:19–20 NLT

Our Savior cries out to us, "Come to me, all you who are weary and burdened, and I will give you rest" (Matthew 11:28 NIV). We may never completely understand why a person takes their own life, but we must understand that it does happen and learn how to respond to it with compassion and grace.

Do People Who Commit Suicide Go to Hell?

Some people believe suicide is an unforgivable or unpardonable sin, but this is not a biblical teaching. God forgives all sin except the sin of rejecting Jesus Christ as Savior and Lord. Yet, I agree with Pastor Harold Warner that this is really not the right question to be asking. Who will apply godly intervention when someone is struggling is the real question.

Do you remember the Philippian jailer in Acts 16? He was going to take his life, because, having lost a prisoner, he would have been executed anyway. "But Paul shouted, 'Don't harm yourself! We are all here!'" (Acts 16:28 NIV). You and I need to be the intervening voice to someone today, just like Paul was to the Philippian jailer, who went from suicidal to saved in the same night.[10] Jesus is the answer to anyone suffering with thoughts of despair.

I have taught the Gospel of Luke at both the graduate and undergraduate levels. In Luke 4, we hear Jesus' sermon and understand his messianic mission: "The Spirit of the LORD is upon Me, because He has anointed Me to preach the gospel to the poor; He has sent Me to heal the brokenhearted, to proclaim liberty to the captives and recovery of sight to the blind, to set at liberty those who are oppressed; to proclaim the acceptable year of the LORD" (Luke 4:18–19 NKJV). The point is, Jesus will set the captives free. He will set at liberty those who are oppressed. Jesus is our peace.

Yes, the salvation we receive from Jesus Christ is eternal, regardless of our mental state or our spiritual maturity or immaturity. Paul the apostle wrote: "In Him you also trusted, after you heard the word of truth, the gospel of your salvation; in whom also, having believed, you were sealed with the Holy Spirit of promise" (Ephesians 1:13 NKJV). A "seal" in biblical times referred to a finished transaction, complete ownership. When we received Christ as Savior, we were, in a sense, locked into God's family by the substitutionary death Jesus Christ endured for us on the cross.

In addition, the Holy Spirit indwelled us at the moment of our salvation, giving us the spiritual capacity to live a life above the power of sin: "Sin shall not have dominion over you, for you are not under law but under grace" (Romans 6:14 NKJV).

Fact: Mental illness is not a character flaw; it is a disease. Mental illness is not a choice, but the good news is that it is treatable.

Fact: Talking intelligently about suicide does not cause suicide, but it can prevent it. Failing to talk about it can have disastrous consequences. You may not be an expert, but your care and compassion are essential, so know the facts and the fallacies about suicide.

Fact: You don't need to help a friend or loved one alone. Make use of mental health professionals, Christian counselors, and conversant pastors.

Fact: Suicide is the second leading cause of death among ten- to nineteen-year-olds. Nationally, we lose more than two thousand children and teens per year. To put that into context, that's another 9/11 body count every eighteen months among our children. It is safe to directly ask your child, "Have you ever considered ending your life?" Speaking to a young person directly about suicide does not increase their risk of suicide, but it does increase the chance they will talk to us and get the help they need.

4. **Mental illness is not a spiritual problem.** One of the principles I learned very early in my ministry is that Christians don't gossip, they just share prayer requests. One reason we do not discuss mental problems in the church is the fear of people gossiping and ostracizing us. We have lost our first love. "By this all men will know that you are my disciples, if you have love for one another" (John

13:35). According to Christian psychologist Dr. Daniel Morehead, "Mental illness is not caused by sin or a lack of faith, and neither is it cured by repentance or increased faith. In the past, some people have been told that they are depressed because they lack faith, or that they don't need mental health treatment, just to practice their faith. We now know that this is wrong, just as wrong as telling someone with a broken leg that they just need faith, and that they should not go to the doctor to get the leg treated."[11] While is certainly true that our spiritual life affects our physical, mental, and emotional life, we must do more than quote a Bible verse at someone who is struggling with depression. The church must practice the ministry of presence with those who are hurting. God's presence works through his people. Let him work through you.

5. **Save the Suicide Prevention Lifeline in your phone contacts: 1-800-273-8255.** This is the number for you to call if you know someone who is struggling, and you need information on how to help. It's also the number to call if you are thinking about suicide. Also, "Like" the National Suicide Prevention Lifeline Facebook page: www.facebook.com/800273TALK. This phenomenal organization interfaces with Facebook to geographically pinpoint suicidal comments on Facebook and intervenes with responses to provide assistance.

I had the honor to spend time with Dr. Steve Warner when I preached at his church in the Boston metro area. We remain friends, and I highly respect his ministry. Dr. Warner recently shared this gripping post on Facebook:

> 1-800-273-8255. This is a number we should all have at hand, if not for ourselves, for others. It is the National Suicide Prevention Hotline. Forty-one years ago today

my father took his own life. I still can't believe it. He had a nervous breakdown, but no one guessed that he was desperate. I still go over the warning signs and only a couple of them apply to him. He was a strong Christian but believers struggle with stuff, too. We live with the fallacy of spiritual perfection—and it can be deadly. So, he suffered in silence. Please, please don't do that. Call someone. Talk. Ask for help. And if you know someone exhibiting symptoms of depression or withdrawal, engage them in conversation. Gently ask questions rather than give pat answers. And don't pontificate. Suffering people need a listening ear, not a wagging tongue. I know this isn't my normal upbeat entry, but you'll pardon me if I'm not feeling it today. I'll be better soon. But some people won't be. So, if I can help save a life today by being open, that is what would make me rejoice. I'm just sad that it won't be my dad's.

6. **Vulnerability is your superpower to save lives.** We're all broken. We're all messed up. We need to share our struggles and begin an open and honest conversation. We need to educate ourselves. Some of the most influential Christians I personally know regularly see Christian counselors and therapists. It is an often-overlooked fact that some of the most effective Christians of all time have had lifelong struggles with depression, thoughts of suicide, and mental illness. You are not alone.

7. **It is not a sin to ask for help—ever! The most important step you can make right now is asking for help.** If you are struggling, stop struggling alone. Pick up the phone and call a trusted friend or a biblical counselor or a local pastor. You do not need to shoulder your burden alone. Remember, the book of Galatians calls us to "carry each other's burdens, and in this way you will fulfill the law of Christ" (6:2 NIV).

The Suicide Epidemic

- One million people worldwide take their lives each year.
- Every fifteen minutes someone commits suicide in the United States.
- Twice as many U.S. citizens kill themselves than kill one another each year.
- One in five completed suicides in the United States involves a war veteran.
- Males take their lives at nearly five times the rate of females and represent more than 80 percent of all U.S. suicides.
- Suicide rates for females are highest among those aged 45–54.
- Suicide is the second-leading cause of death among college students.
- Suicide is the third-leading cause of death among those aged 15–24.
- Suicide is the fourth-leading cause of death among those aged 10–14.
- For every person who takes their life, there are twenty-five attempted suicides.

8. **Provide specific ministry for those suffering from mental illness in the church and in your home.** This is best accomplished through private recovery groups in which those who are living with the same mental illness or pain can gain new friendships and greater understanding. Faithfully and fervently pray for these individuals, believing God can do the impossible. With this godly ambition, we must pray for God's perfect will to be accomplished

(see 1 John 5:14–15). Find a qualified, biblically based counselor or mental health professional who can bring further insight to those suffering from mental illness. Emphasize the power of God's Word to heal the mind, heart, and soul. Read and study the Bible. God's Word is therapeutic for all of us. It is inspired by the Holy Spirit and can calm us in the greatest crisis (see Hebrews 4:12). Read Scripture aloud in your home. Read the Bible when your thoughts are troubled and anxiety seeks to bind you. Watch for ways the Holy Spirit uses the Bible to comfort you in every life situation.

Be Present

Babe Ruth once said, "It's hard to beat a person who never gives up." The church should never give up on, cast aside, or push out the mentally ill. Stephen Altrogge put it like this:

> Until the day Jesus returns, I will live in a body which does not function as God originally intended. My brain, which is a key, central, integral part of my body, will not function correctly. Chemicals will become imbalanced. Serotonin will not be properly absorbed. Norepinephrine will be unevenly distributed. Synapses won't fire correctly. My brain, just like every other part of my body, is prone to illness.[12]

The church needs to be present on the frontlines, ministering to all those who've been afflicted, by implementing a healing equation:

- **Admit that every one of us struggles.** We're all broken. We're all messed up.
- **Love instead of judging or condemning.** One of the reasons we do not discuss mental problems in the church is the fear of people gossiping and ostracizing us.

- **Encourage those struggling with mental illnesses to serve and become involved within our church communities.** Many people struggling with a mental illness are extremely witty, good-humored, and highly intelligent.
- **See ourselves as God sees us.** The most important perspective is applying the truth of God's Word to every situation of our lives and seeing ourselves as God sees us. In Christ we are whole, as forgiven as we will ever be, perfectly loved, and "more than conquerors through him who loved us" (Romans 8:37).

PART 3

PROTECTING YOUR SHALOM IN THE DIFFICULT TIMES

The Unpardonable Sin

What It Is and What It Isn't

I n the classic Western movie *Unforgiven*, Clint Eastwood plays
the starring role of the much-troubled William Munny, a hard-
drinking gunslinger reformed by a good and loving wife. Thanks
to her influence, he gave up whiskey and killing, but after she
dies, Munny and his two young children are destitute. Promised
a substantial reward, Munny is lured back into his former life.
Conflicted, he says to anyone who will listen, "I am not that kind
of man," referring to his former way of life. I am not sure Munny is
convinced, though. Nor do others seem convinced. In the end, William Munny, who's been "lucky in killing," still seems very much
the man he once was and, alas, remains very much unforgiven.

This sad but excellent movie captures a grim and troubling
human reality: Because of our sin, we are plagued by guilt. Thank-
fully, when we find forgiveness in Christ, the guilt is lifted. At
least it is supposed to be. For many, however, guilt clings like a
cheap perfume. Of course, most people are persuaded that past

sins—that is, prior to conversion—are forgiven, but what of grievous sins that are committed *after* conversion? Inexcusable sins— sins that should never have been committed? Even worse, what about sins that seem so wrong, so heinous, that they are regarded as unforgivable, unpardonable? Are there unpardonable sins?

The Bible does speak of certain sins that seem especially egregious. I call these sins "dangerous sins." Let's review the relevant passages of Scripture.

Dangerous Sins

In several passages, the Bible links sin and death. An early example is found in the clash between Moses and Pharaoh. After bringing upon Egypt the plague of locusts, Pharaoh summons Moses and says, "I have sinned against the LORD your God, and against you. Now therefore, forgive my sin, I pray you, only this once, and entreat the LORD your God only to remove this death from me" (Exodus 10:16–17). Given his pagan mindset and worldview, we may not be able to grasp exactly what Pharaoh has said. After all, like all the peoples of the ancient Near East, Pharaoh and the Egyptians were polytheists, whose understanding of the gods was nothing like that of monotheists like Abraham and the patriarchs. What is clear, however, is Pharaoh's linkage of sin and death. My guess is that Pharaoh recognized that in defying the God of Moses, who demonstrated great power in the plague that he brought on Egypt—in defiance of Pharaoh's gods—the God of Moses might strike him dead. So Pharaoh asks Moses—not one of his priests or one of his impotent gods—to forgive his sin and "entreat the LORD," the God of Moses, "to remove this death."

Later, Moses instructs the people of Israel: "The fathers shall not be put to death for the children, nor shall the children be put to death for the fathers; every man shall be put to death for his own sin" (Deuteronomy 24:16). It is clear in this law, as well as in a number of others, that certain sins will result in death. But the death envisioned here is what we call capital punishment. And what is called "sin" here could also be called "crime." Certain crimes, such as murder, will result in death; and this death is at the hands of human judges. This is not death at the hands of God. It is death in reference to temporal life, not in the world to come.

In the story of Elijah and the widow (1 Kings 17:8–24), we find an interesting comment. A fearful widow asks the prophet Elijah, "What have you against me, O man of God? You have come to me to bring my sin to remembrance, and to cause the death of my son!" (1 Kings 17:18). Up to this point in the story, Elijah has been a benefactor and protector of the woman and her young son. Thanks to the prophet, they have not starved to death. But unexpectedly, her son became ill and, apparently, died. The distraught woman concludes—wrongly, of course—that the mere presence of the prophet had made known her sins to God, with the result that she has been punished. It is a warped theology, largely infused with superstition. As it turns out, whatever sins she may have committed, they had nothing to do with the death of her son. The prophet cries out to God, "O Lord my God, let this child's soul come into him again" (v. 21), and he is revived (v. 22). The lad's death and his resuscitation had nothing to do with his mother's sin or righteousness, whatever she herself might have believed.

In the New Testament, sin and death are linked. Paul frequently speaks of sin and death, for the former results in the latter. Before his conversion, Paul's great concern was finding a remedy for sin. Referring to Adam's sin, Paul says, "Therefore as sin came into the world through one man and death through sin, and so death spread to all men because all men sinned" (Romans 5:12). Here, Paul is referring primarily to physical death, to mortality that Adam's sin brought into the world. Thanks to Adam's sin, every human will face infirmity and death. Later, Paul speaks of spiritual death brought on by sin: "Do you not know that if you yield yourselves to any one as obedient slaves, you are slaves of the one whom you obey, either of sin, which leads to death, or of obedience, which leads to righteousness?" (Romans 6:16). A little later, Paul sums up his argument: "For the wages of sin is death, but the free gift of God is eternal life in Christ Jesus our Lord" (Romans 6:23).

This was Paul's great concern—the sin that leads to eternal death. In meeting the risen Christ on the road to Damascus, Paul learned that it was in Christ's death on the cross that sin is forgiven, not in scrupulous observance of "works of law." The wages paid out for sin are death, but God's free gift in Messiah Jesus is eternal life.

James, the brother of Jesus, says something similar. Warning against the workings of lust and temptation, James says, "Then desire when it has conceived gives birth to sin; and sin when it is full-grown brings forth death" (James 1:15).

Jesus also speaks of very dangerous sins. He warns his disciples that "whoever causes one of these little ones who believe in me to sin, it would be better for him to have a great millstone fastened round his neck and to be drowned in the depth of the sea" (Matthew 18:6; cf. Mark 9:42 and Luke 17:2). Interpreters believe Jesus is referring not to recent converts but to children, as the context suggests (Matthew 18:4; cf. Mark 9:37), and perhaps has in mind the shameful way some children were abused (through exposure, sexual trafficking). Especially ominous is what Jesus says of Judas Iscariot the betrayer: "It would have been better for that man if he had not been born" (Matthew 26:24; Mark 14:21).

Two passages in 1 Corinthians and a third in 1 Timothy seem to speak of special, negative consequences that result from sin. The first is in 1 Corinthians 5:1–13, where Paul responds to a report of incest within the church itself. Evidently a man has become sexually involved with his father's wife, which Paul describes as a form of immorality "that is not found even among pagans" (v. 1a). Most interpreters assume that the woman in question is the second wife of the man's father (v. 1b "his father's wife"). Due to death in childbirth, which in late antiquity was all too common, many men remarried, and sometimes their new wives were the same age as sons by the first wives. This reality gave rise to temptation.

Jewish people regarded incest as abhorrent. Perhaps the most notorious example concerned Reuben, Jacob's firstborn son. Reuben had sex with his father's concubine (Genesis 35:22). When Jacob's sons years later gathered around the dying patriarch to hear his final words, Jacob condemned Reuben and denied him his firstborn status (Genesis 49:3–4). In the law of Moses, incest was strictly forbidden (Leviticus 18:7–9), including a man having sex with his stepmother (v. 8: "You shall not uncover the nakedness of your father's wife").

Paul is horrified that incest not only has occurred in the church at Corinth, but that the church doesn't seem too concerned about it. "Ought you not rather to mourn?" Paul asks. "Let him who has done this be removed from among you" (1 Corinthians 5:2). He goes on to say, "I have already pronounced judgment in the name of the Lord Jesus on the man who has done such a thing" (vv. 3–4). The apostle then instructs the church: "You are to deliver this man to Satan for the destruction of his flesh, that his spirit may be saved in the day of the Lord Jesus" (v. 5).

What does it mean "to deliver" someone "to Satan for the destruction of his flesh"? Paul's language reminds us of what God says to Satan in Job 2:6 (according to the Greek version): "I deliver him [Job] to you." Satan destroys the physical health of Job, but not his life. Paul does not speak of "eternal destruction and exclusion from the presence of the Lord," as he does of the wicked in 2 Thessalonians 1:9. The purpose of this "destruction" of the flesh here in 1 Corinthians 5:5 is redemptive: that one's "spirit may be saved in the day of the Lord Jesus." But in what sense is the sinner's flesh destroyed?

The answer to this question is much debated by interpreters. In my view, Paul is talking about the destruction of the flesh's capacity for *pleasure*. This includes "destruction" manifesting itself as sickness and weakness (as we shall see in another example shortly).

I think what Paul says about the results of sexual sin in Romans 1:18–32, where the sin leaves marks on the body, is relevant. The sin here in 1 Corinthians 5 is a fleshly one; the "destruction of the flesh" nullifies the sinful gratification, thus making it possible for the sinner to repent and be restored. The second passage, to be considered now, seems to make the same point.

In his first letter to Timothy, Paul warns of "certain persons (who) have made shipwreck of their faith, among them Hymenaeus and Alexander, whom I have delivered to Satan that they may learn not to blaspheme" (1 Timothy 1:19–20). In this passage, Paul says nothing about immoral behavior, but he uses the same language of delivering an offender to Satan. What will happen to Hymenaeus and Alexander, who "have made shipwreck of their faith," is hard to say. But outside the spiritual protection of the church, these two men will suffer or in some way be harmed. Even so, the result may be positive. Paul says that "they may learn not to blaspheme." Perhaps this means a recovery of faith; perhaps it only means that they will cease in their blasphemies, whether or not their faith recovers.

The third passage supports the approach that I have taken here. In 1 Corinthians 11:27–32, Paul warns believers not to take observance of the Lord's Supper lightly:

> Whoever, therefore, eats the bread or drinks the cup of the Lord in an unworthy manner will be guilty of profaning the body and blood of the Lord. Let a man examine himself, and so eat of the bread and drink of the cup. For any one who eats and drinks without discerning the body eats and drinks judgment upon himself. That is why many of you are weak and ill, and some have died. But if we judged ourselves truly, we should not be judged. But when we are judged by the Lord, we are chastened so that we may not be condemned along with the world.

The wider context of this passage suggests that some Corinthians were treating the Lord's Supper as a drunken feast. They may have done this because of their pagan background, in which people were invited to feasts in honor of this god or that god. At this feast, devotees may well have eaten much and drunk even more. Indeed, in the pagan religious culture, drunkenness could be seen as a sign of spiritual intoxication, in the belief that in drinking wine (a gift of the god Dionysius) one was drinking in the spirit of the deity. In his exhortation to the Ephesians, Paul seems to be making this very comparison, when he says, "Do not get drunk with wine, for that is debauchery; but be filled with the Spirit" (Ephesians 5:18). It may well be that some in the Corinthian church thought that drinking to the point of intoxication, perhaps even carousing, was a legitimate way to celebrate the Lord's Supper. *If Dionysius was so honored, why shouldn't Christ be honored in the same way?* But such behavior is not evidence of being filled with the Spirit; it is the opposite.

Paul warns against "profaning the body and blood of the Lord" (1 Corinthians 11:27). If one does so, one "eats and drinks judgment upon himself" (v. 29). Apparently, some of the Corinthians have done this, which is why, Paul says, "many of you are weak and ill, and some have died" (v. 30). But even in sickness and death, the goal is redemptive: "When we are judged by the Lord, we are chastened so that we may not be condemned along with the world" (v. 32). When Paul is speaking of the condemnation of the world, he is speaking of final, eternal judgment. Paul is saying that weakness and illness in some cases are judgments from God, intended to save offenders from a far worse judgment.

Restoration seems to be the theme that unites all three of these passages that speak of what I call "dangerous" sins. In the first passage, focused on the sin of incest, Paul speaks of fearful judgment. But the purpose of this judgment is "that [the sinner's] spirit may be saved" (1 Corinthians 5:5). In the second passage, which refers to ruined faith and blasphemy, the purpose of judgment is to "learn not to blaspheme" (1 Timothy 1:20), while in the third passage, which is focused on the profanation of the Lord's Supper, the resulting judgment is seen as a chastening whose purpose is to avoid condemnation (1 Corinthians 11:32).

The lesson seems to be that some types of sin are especially egregious and elicit divine punishment, punishment that can take the form of physical illness, even death. But even so, the judgment is seen as a form of chastening, whose purpose is redemptive and restorative.

I have reviewed three dangerous sins. They are dangerous, to be sure, but I think ultimately God's response to them is redemptive. I now turn to three passages that warn of what I call "deadly sins." Are these unpardonable, unforgiveable sins?

"Deadly Sins"

Often behind the debate about the "unpardonable sin" is the question that asks if people can fall away from the faith. Some answer in the affirmative. Others say no: "once saved, always saved," as the saying goes. The conflicting answers are usually tied to larger, competing theological perspectives, such as Calvinism and Arminianism. In my view, apostasy is not only possible, but is clearly taught in Scripture. Let us consider a few of the most relevant passages.

In the parable of the sower (Mark 4:3–20), in which the various responses to the proclamation of the Good News of the kingdom are illustrated, Jesus describes people who "endure for a while" (v. 17), then after experiencing opposition "they stumble" (v. 17 NKJV), or, as the RSV translates, "they fall away" (Mark 4:17). In speaking of the future and the troubles it will bring, Jesus warns his disciples that "false prophets will arise and lead many astray," and that the person "who endures to the end will be saved" (Matthew 24:11, 13). These passages (and others) suggest that some people who initially believe in Jesus and belong to the church could leave the faith.

Several warnings of apostasy are found in the New Testament. Paul speaks of a general apostasy when the "man of lawlessness" appears (2 Thessalonians 2:3). Paul is referring to the Antichrist (as in 1 John 2:18), the archenemy of God and the church. The word *apostasy* comes from the Greek *apostasia*, which means "to fall away" or "to abandon the faith."

In his letters to Pastor Timothy, Paul warned his colleague: "Now the Spirit expressly says that in later times some will depart from the faith by giving heed to deceitful spirits and doctrines of demons" (1 Timothy 4:1). Paul further exhorts Timothy, "Take heed to yourself and to your teaching; hold to that, for by so doing you will save both yourself and your hearers" (4:16); "for some have already strayed after Satan" (5:15). It is likely that Paul here refers to people who have abandoned the faith altogether. It is possible the same is true in 2 Timothy 4:10, when Paul refers to "Demas, in love with this present world, has deserted me."

The author of the book of Hebrews offers several warnings against abandoning the faith, including: "If we sin deliberately after receiving the knowledge of the truth, there no longer remains a sacrifice for sins" (10:26). Three verses later comes this question: "How much worse punishment do you think will be deserved by the man who has spurned the Son of God, and profaned the blood of the covenant by which he was sanctified, and outraged the Spirit of grace?" (10:29). He concludes this grim chapter on a note of encouragement, suggesting that "we are not of those who shrink back and are destroyed, but of those who have faith and keep their souls" (10:39).

James advises his readers: "My brethren, if any one among you wanders from the truth and some one brings him back, let him know that whoever brings back a sinner from the error of his way will save his soul from death and will cover a multitude of sins" (James 5:19–20). Sound advice, in light of Peter's warning: "For if, after they have escaped the defilements of the world through the knowledge of our Lord and Savior Jesus Christ, they are again entangled in them and overpowered, the last state has become worse for them than the first. For it would have been better for them never to have known the way of righteousness than after knowing it to turn back from the holy commandment delivered to them" (2 Peter 2:20–21).

Speaking in Revelation, the last book of the Bible, the risen Jesus warns his followers: "I am coming soon; hold fast what you have, so that no one may seize your crown" (Revelation 3:11). In this context, having one's "crown seized" means losing one's place in the community of the redeemed and therefore losing one's right to admission into the kingdom of God.

Other passages could be cited, but I think these are sufficient to make the point that Jesus and the writers of the New Testament believed that people could, and some people would, abandon the faith. Evidence of this possibility is seen all around us today, as clergy and laity alike give up the faith and say they no longer believe in Jesus or in God. Their reasons for abandoning the faith may vary, but their explicit expressions of de-conversion reflect real apostasy and should be taken seriously.

What concerns me most in the present chapter are passages of Scripture that some think speak of sins for which no forgiveness can ever be obtained. After all, it is one thing for a person to decide to abandon the faith; it is quite another for a person to do something for which he believes he can never be forgiven and never be brought into a right relationship with God. In short, I am asking if there are sins that result in a certain and unavoidable sentence to hell. There are three passages that speak of these potentially deadly sins. Let's review them.

The first passage that some think speaks of an unpardonable sin is found in Mark 3. In this context, Jesus has been accused of being in league with Satan, or, as this evil being was also known, Beelzebul. Jesus was so successful in healing and casting out evil spirits, some scholars accused him: "He is possessed by Beelzebul, and by the prince of demons he casts out the demons" (v. 22). The charge was not only unfair and insulting, it was dangerous. In Jewish society, sorcery—a clear violation of the Law of Moses—could be punished with death (Deuteronomy 13:1–11).

Jesus retorts that if Satan is casting out Satan, then he is in big trouble. His dominion will collapse, and he himself will come to an end (Mark 3:23–26). Jesus goes on to teach that he has bound the "strong man" (i.e., Satan) and is now plundering his house (v. 27), by which Jesus means he is liberating people who had been in bondage to Satan. Every exorcism meant the setting free of someone who had been held captive. It is in this context that Jesus warns his accusers: "'Truly, I say to you, all sins will be forgiven the sons of men, and whatever blasphemies they utter; but whoever blasphemes against the Holy Spirit never has forgiveness, but is guilty of an eternal sin'—for they had said, 'He has an unclean spirit'" (vv. 28–30; cf. Matthew 12:31–32; Luke 12:10).

What Jesus is talking about here is the rejection of his mission and person. When a critic or objector "blasphemes against the Holy Spirit," he has rejected the Holy Spirit's work of testifying to Jesus (cf. John 5:32; 8:18; 15:26: "the Spirit of truth . . . will bear witness to me"). In essence, this "eternal sin," for which one "never has forgiveness," is the rejection of Jesus. The Holy Spirit's witness to Jesus is attributed to Satan.

Jesus is not talking about a sin that a believer may inadvertently or even intentionally commit. He is talking about a willful and very evil rejection of the testimony of the Holy Spirit, with regard to Jesus. To assert that the work of the Holy Spirit is the work of Satan, the most unclean and evil spirit of all, is not only blasphemy, but a rejection of Jesus and his saving Gospel. Note, too, that the men who accused Jesus of being in league with Satan were theologians who should have known what they were talking about. The scholars who criticized Jesus willfully and maliciously identified the work of the Holy Spirit in Jesus as the work of Satan.

The second passage is found in 1 John 5, where the author counsels his readers: "If any one sees his brother committing what is not a mortal sin, he will ask, and God will give him life for those whose sin is not mortal. There is sin which is mortal; I do not say that one is to pray for that" (v. 16). What "mortal" sin the author has in mind is not obvious. It may well be the type of sin Paul talks about above, whose consequences lead to illness and death.

In those cases, the purpose of the illness was to spare the sinner the consequences of eternal death. But here in 1 John, intercessory prayer is limited to those who commit "what is not a mortal sin." The "sin which is mortal" is something else.

So what is the sin "which is mortal" (lit. "that leads to death"), for which one is not to intercede in prayer? Before answering this question, it will help to consider the larger context of Scripture. As strange as it may seem, there are passages in the Old Testament in which God commands his prophet not to pray for his people. The most jarring example of this is found in Jeremiah 7. Israel's sin is so egregious that it can only be viewed as complete apostasy. God says to Jeremiah: "Do not pray for this people, or lift up cry or prayer for them, and do not intercede with me, for I do not hear you" (Jeremiah 7:16). In Isaiah 6, God is so angry, he urges the people not to repent, lest they be healed (Isaiah 6:9–10). In short, Israel has committed a sin that leads to death, and the prophet is not to intercede on the nation's behalf.

I believe, along with a number of interpreters, that what the author of 1 John is talking about is the rejection of Jesus as Messiah and as Son of God, a sin, or lie, that the author of 1 John warns about elsewhere in his letter (e.g., 1 John 2:22; 4:3). Accordingly, the sin that leads to death is the rejection of Jesus. The sin of which 1 John speaks is in essence the same as the sin that Jesus was talking about in Mark 3.

The third passage is found in Hebrews 6. It is a complicated and much disputed passage. It will help to cite all of it:

> For it is impossible to restore again to repentance those who have once been enlightened, who have tasted the heavenly gift, and have become partakers of the Holy Spirit, and have tasted the goodness of the word of God and the powers of the age to come, if they then commit apostasy, since they crucify the Son of God on their own account and hold him up to contempt. For land which has drunk the rain that often falls upon it, and brings forth vegetation useful

to those for whose sake it is cultivated, receives a blessing from God. But if it bears thorns and thistles, it is worthless and near to being cursed; its end is to be burned.

Hebrews 6:4–8

What readers find shocking are the opening the words: "it is impossible to restore again to repentance" (v. 4). The author is speaking of apostasy, as is made clear in verse 6. All else in this passage explains why restoration is impossible. It needs to be made clear that the author of Hebrews is not talking about a particular sin; he is only speaking of apostasy (cf. Hebrews 3:12) and warning of its dire consequences. Yet, this passage in Hebrews does correlate with the passages in Mark 3 and 1 John 5 that we have reviewed.

In Mark 3, Jesus specifies an unpardonable sin, which is to misidentify the work of the Holy Spirit as the work of Satan. In 1 John 5, the author speaks of a sin that "leads to death," which is rejecting Jesus and his work. In Hebrews 6, the author warns that apostasy entails holding Jesus up to "contempt," which again implies a complete rejection of Jesus and his saving work.

These three passages are frightening, to be sure, but they are not talking about the kinds of sin, including terrible sins, that people commit. The person who seeks forgiveness is not the person who has committed "the unpardonable sin." The person who commits the unpardonable sin seeks no forgiveness. Repenting and repudiating Jesus are polar opposites. That's what makes sin unpardonable, unforgivable. He or she doesn't want forgiveness; doesn't want what God freely offers.

Forgiveness and Hope

The theme that runs throughout the Bible is God's love for humanity and his redemptive plan. God desires our restoration and reconciliation. Closely related to this theme is God's willingness to hear us and forgive us. God does so, because one of his primary characteristics is his grace. Here are a few examples: After his sins of adultery and murder, King David petitions God, "Purge me with hyssop, and I shall be clean; wash me, and I shall be whiter than snow" (Psalm 51:7). God hears and David's sins are "put away" (2 Samuel 12:13). Similarly, through Isaiah the prophet, God reaches out to sinful, rebellious Israel: "Come now, let us reason together, says the LORD: though your sins are like scarlet, they shall be as white as snow; though they are red like crimson, they shall become like wool" (Isaiah 1:18). One hundred years later God speaks again to sinful Israel, this time through Jeremiah: "I will forgive their iniquity, and I will remember their sin no more" (Jeremiah 31:34; quoted in Hebrews 8:12; 10:17). In very poetic terms, the psalmist says of God's forgiving grace: "For as the heavens are high above the earth, so great is his steadfast love toward those who fear him; as far as the east is from the west, so far does he remove our transgressions from us" (Psalm 103:11–12).

God's forgiving grace was not lost on the rabbis, who knew the Old Testament Scriptures inside and out. The rabbis were remembered to have said, "There is nothing greater than repentance," for it will also result in forgiveness (*Sipre Deut*. 2.24 [on Deuteronomy 4:30]). Neither was God's forgiving grace lost on the Rabbi from Galilee, Jesus of Nazareth. Jesus told the paralyzed man, whom he was about to heal, "Your sins are forgiven" (Mark 2:5). He tells the sinful woman, "Your sins are forgiven" (Luke 7:48). The risen Jesus commanded his apostles to proclaim repentance and forgiveness of sins in his name (Luke 24:47); and they did so (Acts 5:31; 10:43; 13:38; 26:18). The rabbis said that repentance was so effective it could cancel a divine decree of judgment (*b. Yoma* 86b: "God cancels his own words for the sake of repentance"). The apostle Paul said the same thing, affirming that in Christ God nailed the decree against humanity to the cross (Colossians 2:13–14).

Apart from rejecting Christ, whose death on the cross makes forgiveness possible, no sin is unforgivable. God will forgive murderers, thieves, adulterers, even hypocrites! God never closes the door on anyone who repents. God fully understands our weaknesses—physical, mental, and emotional. No one is beyond God's redemptive reach, not even the one who takes his own life (and suicide, by the way, is not the unpardonable sin). This is why it is so important to let go of guilt. Please know that you can have forgiveness. Don't allow guilt to consume you. Guilt is a cancer; untreated, it will eat you up. Let a loving and forgiving God nail it to the cross of Christ. Why should you pay for what he has already paid?

The Greeks and Romans of late antiquity had no hope. They went to their deaths in sorrow and despair. I have read many ancient epitaphs. They are so sad. One reads: "Heartless death carried you off, tender child."[1] Another asks, "What are we? A man . . . now no more. Just the stone and inscription remain."[2] Another asserts, "Nothing of my life endures";[3] while another laments, "You parents' hopes reduced to mockery!"[4] The epitaphs of Christians read much differently, affirming confidence that deceased loved ones are in the presence of God: "Here lies Artemia . . . she departed to Christ . . . into the heavenly kingdom";[5] "Here lies Martianus. . . . He has gone to God."[6]

Our hope as humans lies in the grace and mercy of God. That he loves us and wishes to redeem us is seen in the death of his Son. If God loves us this much, there is no reason for despair. All sin can be forgiven; every sinner can be restored.

Mind Wars

Taking Every Thought Captive

Walking through the British Museum in London a few years ago, I was struck by the impressive stone reliefs produced by the ancient Assyrians. The reliefs depict the capture of enemy fortresses and the defeat of their defenders. The Assyrians, whose Near Eastern empire reached its zenith in the eighth century BC, used grappling hooks and ropes to pull down the stone walls of fortresses and walled cities. The grappling hook caught the top tier of the stones, men and horses pulled on the rope, and stones were dislodged and toppled. They did this again and again until the wall was low enough that troops could enter the city.

Capturing Thoughts

The apostle Paul, who, until he met the risen Jesus Christ on the road to Damascus, was an enemy of Jesus and his church, was familiar with the battle tactics illustrated in the ancient Assyrian reliefs, even if he had never actually seen them. He used this military tactic in his graphic imagery in order to put some teeth in his exhortation that the Christians of Corinth must discipline their minds:

> For though we live in the world we are not carrying on a worldly war, for the weapons of our warfare are not worldly but have divine power to destroy strongholds. We destroy arguments and every proud obstacle to the knowledge of God, and take every thought captive to obey Christ, being ready to punish every disobedience, when your obedience is complete.
>
> 2 Corinthians 10:3–6

I love this passage. It is one of the passages that shaped my own thinking as I conceived and designed the Christian Thinkers Society. The Christian faith is not supposed to be gullible belief in whatever somebody asserts. It is supposed to be a hard-thinking, critical-thinking faith. Our thoughts are supposed to be generous, and we are supposed to be open-minded. But we are not supposed to be credulous and naïve.

Let's look carefully at every element in 2 Corinthians 10:3–6. When we do, you will see why I think this passage is so important. First, Paul notes that "though we live in the world we are not carrying on a worldly war." This reminds us of what Jesus, in the custody of Pontius Pilate, prefect of Samaria and Judea, told the governor: "My kingship is not of this world; if my kingship were of this world, my servants would fight, that I might not be handed over to the Jews; but my kingship is not from the world" (John 18:36). I think it is very probable that Paul knew of this teaching and was alluding to it when he wrote to the Corinthians.

Jesus and his followers were very much aware of those Jewish men during the time of Herod the Great (ruled 37–4 BC), or right after Herod's death, who claimed to be a prophet or messiah and claimed they could liberate Israel and bring in the awaited time of redemption and blessing. Or so they promised. Each one was defeated, and many died. Even in the early years of the church, several men in Israel claimed to be prophets or messianic kings. The prophets were hunted down and killed. The messianic kings raised armies and attacked Herod, or his sons who succeeded him, or the Romans themselves. Indeed, it was the rise of at least three of these would-be royal messiahs that ensured the Roman capture of Jerusalem and destruction of its beautiful temple in the year 70 AD. Jesus and his followers were not interested in this kind of messianic "liberation."

This is why Jesus responded the way he did when Pilate asked him, "Are you the King of the Jews?" (John 18:33). Pilate's interrogation of Jesus was not simply to determine guilt and punishment, but to gather intel. The worried governor wanted to know what he was up against. He was in Jerusalem for the Passover holiday, and his troop strength was far from overwhelming. (Most of his troops were stationed several miles way at Caesarea Maritima, on the Mediterranean coast, where the governor normally resided.) Pilate would have had with him no more than one cohort of Roman legionnaires—about two thousand men—which were not nearly enough to take on a large, angry Jewish army of locals determined to overthrow the authority of the ruling priests and their Roman allies.

As it turned out, Pilate had nothing to worry about. Jesus has no army. His followers have no plans to overthrow anybody. Jesus is a king, to be sure, but his "kingship is not of this world," so his followers won't be doing any fighting, at least not in the conventional, worldly sense. In agreement with this teaching, Paul reminded the Corinthians that "we are not carrying on a worldly war." Followers of Jesus love their enemies and those who persecute them; they don't attack and try to kill them.

What the RSV translates as "not carrying on a worldly war" is literally "we fight not according to the flesh." That may sound peculiar to us moderns, but it had a very serious and very obvious meaning to Paul and his contemporaries. The phrase "according to the flesh" would have been understood as the opposite of "according to the spirit." That is, Paul was thinking of the contrast between flesh and spirit, a contrast that appears elsewhere in his writings. Paul states this reality explicitly in his letter to the Christians of Rome: "To set the mind on the flesh is death, but to set the mind on the Spirit is life and peace" (Romans 8:6). This passage is very relevant for understanding 2 Corinthians 10:3–6.

The Jewish world of Paul's day very much thought in terms of these opposing forces. They also thought of these opposing forces as very much at war with one another. I can illustrate this by simply quoting the opening lines of the well-known War Scroll from Qumran, the ancient site on the northwest shore of the Dead Sea. The scroll begins with these words:

> For the Instructor, the *Rule of the War*. The beginning of the dominion of the Sons of Light shall be undertaken against the forces of the Sons of Darkness, the army of Belial: the troops of Edom, Moab, the sons of Ammon, the Amalekites, Philistia and the troops of the Kittim of Assyria. Supporting them are those who have violated the covenant. The sons of Levi, the sons of Judah, and the sons of Benjamin, those exiled to the wilderness, shall fight against them with [. . .] against all their troops, when the exiles of the Sons of Light return from the Wilderness of the Peoples to camp in the Wilderness of Jerusalem.
>
> 1QM 1:1–3, WAC[1]

This passage beautifully illustrates the flesh-versus-spirit imagery we find from Paul and other New Testament writers. This text, which calls itself the *Rule of the War*, was written for the "Instructor." It is the textbook that was to be used for teaching the members of the community (which most scholars identify with the group called the Essenes, the "doers" of the Covenant) in how to prepare for and conduct the great eschatological battle that will pitch the "Sons of Light" (i.e., the Essenes) against the "Sons of Darkness" (i.e., the Romans and apostate Jews who support the Romans). Note that the "Sons of Darkness" are identified as the "army of Belial." Belial is a name for Satan himself! A great war is envisioned when the Sons of Light return from the wilderness "to camp in the Wilderness of Jerusalem." This probably envisions a siege and eventual recapture of Jerusalem. What is anticipated here is not simply a spiritual conflict of sorts, but an all-out war, in which God's enemies will be killed.

This kind of hope and imagination was in the air during the time of Jesus and his followers (who also refer to "sons of light"; cf. Luke 16:8; John 12:36; 1 Thessalonians 5:5). This same kind of hope also energized many would-be prophets and messiahs who called for revolution. So you can see why Pilate wanted to know what kind of king Jesus was and what kind of following he had. But Jesus envisioned a spiritual battle of far greater consequence than Pilate or his emperor could have imagined. This was Paul's understanding, too. The spiritual problems and realities of Israel and humanity in general would not be resolved by fighting wars with the Romans, which is why Paul wrote:

> Put on the whole armor of God, that you may be able to stand against the wiles of the devil. For we are not contending against flesh and blood, but against the principalities, against the powers, against the world rulers of this present darkness, against the spiritual hosts of wickedness in the heavenly places.
>
> Ephesians 6:11–12

Armed against Enemy Thoughts

This is also why Paul says in 2 Corinthians 10:4 that "the weapons of our warfare are not worldly but have divine power." That is, our weapons are not the physical, literal weapons that Roman troops carry, such as their well-known *gladius*, or short sword. The real weapons are spiritual. In Ephesians 6, Paul describes some of those weapons, including the whole armor of God, the breastplate of righteousness, the shield of faith, the helmet of salvation, and the sword of the Spirit.

The purpose of these spiritual weapons, sourced in the very power of God, Paul says in 2 Corinthians 10:4, is "to destroy strongholds." This is, of course, what every army must do if it is to capture a city. Years later, in 70 AD, the Roman army will do just that; it will capture Jerusalem, one of the greatest strongholds of late antiquity. But Paul envisions capturing the strongholds of Satan and his spiritual allies. Again, Paul's language seems to echo the earlier teaching of Jesus, when he (Jesus) says in response to his critics, "No one can enter a strong man's house and plunder his goods, unless he first binds the strong man; then indeed he may plunder his house" (Mark 3:27). Jesus is that One who is stronger than the "strong man" (Satan), and he has broken into the strong man's house, bound the strong man, and plundered his house. Paul believes that in a sense that is what Jesus' followers must also do: They must destroy fortresses that house and protect that which is evil and potentially harmful.

In 2 Corinthians 10:5, Paul says the believer must "destroy arguments and every proud obstacle to the knowledge of God." Humanity's greatest sins are almost always inspired by pride. The sin of Adam and Eve was rooted in pride—in the misguided belief that they should acquire great knowledge and be like God (Genesis 3:4–5). It is not for nothing that the wise man warned, "Pride goes before destruction, and a haughty spirit before a fall" (Proverbs 16:18). Closely related to pride is the sin of covetousness, a sin expressly forbidden as the last of the Ten Commandments (Exodus 20:17). One of the most dramatic and tragic examples of the bitter fruit that can result from the sin of coveting is seen in King Ahab who coveted Naboth's vineyard. His desire for the vineyard led to false witness, slander, murder, and theft (1 Kings 21:1–14) and eventually Ahab's death (1 Kings 22:34–38).

But it isn't enough simply to destroy harmful arguments and proud obstacles; it is necessary, in a very positive way, to "take every thought captive to obey Christ." In Romans, Paul speaks of the believer setting his mind on the things of the Spirit (Romans 8:5). This is the same idea here. Paul exhorts believers to "pray constantly" (1 Thessalonians 5:17) and to "let the word of Christ dwell in you richly" (Colossians 3:16). If one is vigilant in prayer and one is saturated with the word, or teaching, of Christ, then it is not too hard to "take every thought captive."

But if we don't take our thoughts captive, they will take us captive. In an era of crass materialism, hedonism, pornography, and the like, an undisciplined mind is very vulnerable to temptation. It is like an unguarded bank vault whose door is left open. I am reminded of what pastor Josh Howerton once tweeted: "I preached on detoxing our thoughts from 2 Corinthians 10, 'Take every thought captive' this week, and someone said *it didn't apply because that passage was written about the teaching of false prophets.* Yes, but I've got a false prophet in my own head."[2] I have no doubt he does (as we all do), and that false prophet can only be silenced by smothering him with the word of Christ and a mind set on the things of the Spirit.

It is so important to tell ourselves the truth, to break the cycle of lies and self-deception. One of my favorite books is Scott Peck's *People of the Lie.* It deepened my understanding of how deceitful human beings can be and how harmful mendacity is for both physical as well as mental and psychological health. The antidote to deceit is the Spirit of truth, for "when the Spirit of truth comes, he will guide you into all the truth" (John 16:13).

When Paul speaks of "being ready to punish every disobedience, when your obedience is complete" (2 Corinthians 10:6), he is speaking of self-discipline, or refusing to tolerate self-indulgence. Self-indulgence usually means giving in to coveting what others have. In our materialistic age, this is all too common. We mistakenly think that if we have more _____ (and we can fill in the blank with countless things), we will be satisfied. The spirit of this age proclaims this false message every day. It is simply not true. More stuff will not make us happy.

But what about those sneaky thoughts that surreptitiously pop into our minds unbidden? When an angry, jealous, impure, or covetous thought comes to mind, is that a sin? Is it a failure to "take captive every thought"? Unbidden thoughts are better known as intrusive thoughts, and every single person has them. Yes, everyone.

Even Jesus, who never sinned, experienced intrusive thoughts. For example, Satan tempted Jesus by taking him to a high mountain and showing him "all the kingdoms of the world and the glory of them" (Matthew 4:8). I want to say this clearly: We have no idea what Jesus saw, but he would have seen a lot. This was Satan's greatest temptation of Jesus, used in his attempt to stop the Messianic program of redemption. Satan then commanded Jesus to "fall down and worship me" (Matthew 4:9). My point is, the intrusive thought was placed in Jesus' mind, but from what we can tell from Scripture, he immediately dismissed the intrusive thought of worshiping Satan. Jesus then quoted Deuteronomy 6:13, and Satan left him. All of this reminds me of a quote from pastor Rick Warren: "You are not responsible for the thoughts Satan puts in your mind, but you are responsible for what you do with them."[3] Dr. Charles Stanley concurs: "A thought itself is not a sin. Entertaining a thought and acting out a thought can be sinful. Thoughts come—and it is what we do with those thoughts that matters."[4] The teaching of Jesus' brother James makes it clear that our desiring a thought is what leads to sin: "Then desire when it has conceived gives birth to sin" (James 1:15).

A smart discipline to remember is, "Don't believe everything you think!" Think critically. Psychologist Adam Grant drives the point home with this practical advice: "A sign of wisdom is not believing everything you think. A sign of emotional intelligence is not internalizing everything you feel. Thoughts and emotions are possibilities to entertain, not certainties to take for granted. Question them before you accept them."[5]

So, is being tempted itself a sin? Some people think it is. I don't think so. As we just learned, not only was Jesus himself tempted by Satan before he began his public ministry of preaching and healing, but Jesus taught his disciples to pray that they not be left vulnerable to temptation (Matthew 6:13; Luke 11:4). Jesus also taught that temptations are unavoidable (Matthew 18:7; Luke 22:40).

In 1 Corinthians 10:13, the apostle Paul reinforced the truth that temptations are common. That same verse, however, includes this promise: "God is faithful, and he will not let you be tempted beyond your strength, but with the temptation will also provide the way of escape, that you may be able to endure it." James also warned his readers not to blame God for temptations; God doesn't tempt anyone (James 1:13).

The problem comes when the temptation finds a place at home in your thoughts—as, again, James warns (James 1:14). If you allow a tempting thought—an impure desire, anger, whatever it might be—to take up permanent residence in your mind, that is when you are no longer taking captive every thought to obey Christ. That is when you are no longer putting your mind on the Spirit. An impure thought or a temptation to do wrong, if allowed to linger, may well lead to a sinful deed or word. It isn't the temptation that is the sin; it's the yielding to it, the acting on it.

When bad thoughts pop into your mind, tell them to take a hike. That's what Jesus did when Satan tempted him. Jesus didn't think it over; he didn't imagine what it might be like. No, he said, "Begone, Satan," and Satan departed (Matthew 4:10). But if you do yield to temptation and sin, ask for forgiveness and you will receive it (Jeremiah 31:34; Luke 7:47–48).

Developing the Mind

The aged Moses admonished the second-generation Israelites, soon to enter the Promised Land: "Hear, O Israel: The LORD our God is one LORD; and you shall love the LORD your God with all your heart, and with all your soul, and with all your might. And these words which I command you this day shall be upon your heart" (Deuteronomy 6:4–6). I sometimes paraphrase verse 5 as: "You shall love the LORD your God with all you are and all you have." Jesus paraphrased this important passage, too, when a scholar asked him what the greatest commandment was. Jesus answered: "Hear, O Israel: The Lord our God, the Lord is one; and you shall love the Lord your God with all your heart, and with all your soul, and with all your mind, and with all your strength" (Mark 12:29–30).

Compare Jesus' version with the original version found in Deuteronomy 6, which mentions three elements: all your heart, all your soul, all your might. The first two refer to you; the last element refers to your resources. But notice that Jesus in Mark 12 refers to *four* elements, not three: all your heart, all your soul, all your mind, and all your strength. The first two—heart and soul—match the first two in Deuteronomy. The last one—strength—matches the last one in Deuteronomy. Jesus' reference to "all your mind" is the fourth element, the outlier.

Jesus' expansion does not contradict Deuteronomy in any way; it supplements it. In the Hebrew language and culture, the words for "heart" (*lebav*) and "soul" (*nephesh*) imply thought and will, not emotion only. But the Hebrew text of Deuteronomy does tilt toward emotion and loyalty, which is not surprising, given that Moses' command begins with the words "You shall love the Lord." But Jesus' addition of "all your mind" does alter the complexion of the command somewhat. The Greek word for "mind" (*dianoia*) refers to mind, thought, and intention, not so much loyalty or affection. The word *dianoia* is found in the Gospel of Mark, which is written in Greek. The Aramaic-speaking Jesus probably used the Aramaic word *manda'* ("thought," "knowledge") or *manda'ta'* ("disposition"), in addition to the Aramaic words *lib* ("heart") and *naphesh* ("soul"), which correspond to the Hebrew words that appear in Deuteronomy.

Jesus' appeal to thought or mind should not surprise. In fact, it explains a lot. The Christian movement quickly developed into an intellectual movement, a movement of thinkers. To be sure, personal piety and compassion for the poor and sick were hallmarks of the Christian church. But early Christians were keenly interested in the intellectual dimension of their faith. A body of articulate teaching quickly emerged, which led to theological dialogue and an ever-expanding body of literature. Whereas rabbinic Judaism focused on exactly how to keep the Law of Moses (as seen in the foundational works called the Mishnah and the Talmud), early Christian thinkers pondered exactly how to understand God and his work in Christ.

It is not surprising that Christian apologetics appeared side by side with evangelism. Beginning with the apostles themselves and then continuing with their disciples, the Good News of Jesus and the Resurrection was proclaimed. That was the evangelistic message. But right alongside was the defense of this message, because in both the Jewish synagogue and in the pagan Roman Empire, the idea that humanity's Savior was a crucified Messiah seemed at best odd and at worst downright silly. Vigorous thought was needed, not only to defend the truth of the Good News but to guard against the many false ideas embraced by many in late antiquity.

Remember, in the pagan world there were many gods, yet not one of them was lovable or trustworthy. The gods of the pagans were capricious, fickle, and sometimes dangerous. The gods of the pagans behaved like, well, pagans. The gods of the pagans had no morals, couldn't be trusted, were vengeful, and were often jealous of humans. The only thing about the gods that impressed the pagans was that they were immortal and powerful. The suffering of Jesus on the cross and his ignoble death struck most pagans as the exact opposite of what a divine being should experience. No god in the pagan world would ever suffer on behalf of or in place of a human. Such an idea was absurd.

The pagan mind was addled with irrational thoughts, fears, and oppressive, nagging superstitions. Jews who became believers in Jesus had a much easier time of it, for they had all along believed in the God of Israel and had been instructed by Israel's ancient Scriptures. They knew what truth was, and they knew the God of Abraham was a loving, faithful God. But pagans who became believers in Jesus had much falsehood and nonsense to shed. Their heads were a mental swamp. This is why it was so important for them to become thinkers, to acquire knowledge and to know the truth fully. This is why the apostle Paul emphasizes putting the mind on the Spirit, or, in the words of the fourth evangelist, the "Spirit of truth."

The importance of the mind is anchored in Israel's ancient Scriptures. One immediately thinks of the wisdom offered by Solomon and his court:

Incline your ear, and hear the words of the wise, and apply your mind to my knowledge. (Proverbs 22:17)

Apply your mind to instruction and your ear to words of knowledge. (Proverbs 23:12)

Hear, my son, and be wise, and direct your mind in the way. (Proverbs 23:19)

The wise will heed this sage advice. The wise person will "hear the words of the wise." He or she will "apply [his/her] mind to instruction" and hear instruction. When I read these words, I am reminded of the great old hymn by Kenneth Downie, "In Perfect Peace," based on Isaiah 26:3 (KJV): "Thou wilt keep him in perfect peace, whose mind is stayed on thee." How true this is. If someone has no peace, I doubt their mind is focused on God.

The intelligent, thinking mind is saturated with God's thoughts. The foolish, unthinking mind is caught up with idolatry and polytheism.

Read what the prophet Isaiah says about the idolater who cuts up a piece of wood, part of which he burns in a fire:

> And the rest of it he makes into a god, his idol; and falls down to it and worships it; he prays to it and says, "Deliver me, for thou art my god!" They know not, nor do they discern; for he has shut their eyes, so that they cannot see, and their minds, so that they cannot understand. No one considers, nor is there knowledge or discernment to say, "Half of it I burned in the fire, I also baked bread on its coals, I roasted flesh and have eaten; and shall I make the residue of it an abomination? Shall I fall down before a block of wood?" He feeds on ashes; a deluded mind has led him astray, and he cannot deliver himself.
>
> Isaiah 44:17–20

This would be funny if it were not so tragic—and it is only part of the passage. The pagan carves up a piece of wood, then falls down before it, worships it, and cries out to it begging for deliverance. But the main point here is that the prophet says the foolish idolater has been led astray by his "deluded mind" (v. 20). The idolator stupidly worships a piece of wood. This is a mind not set on the Spirit or guided by the truth of God. This is a mind suffering from spiritual disease.

Regarding these pagans, Paul says:

> Ever since the creation of the world his invisible nature, namely, his eternal power and deity, has been clearly perceived in the things that have been made. So they are without excuse; for although they knew God they did not honor him as God or give thanks to

him, but they became futile in their thinking and their senseless minds were darkened. Claiming to be wise, they became fools, and exchanged the glory of the immortal God for images resembling mortal man or birds or animals or reptiles.

Romans 1:20–23

Paul is writing more than seven centuries after the time of Isaiah. Although it is disputed, interpreters think he was thinking of human history down to his own day. Certainly, what he says in the passage above describes perfectly the Greco-Roman world of his time, as well as humans much, much earlier. I could have quoted more of Romans 1, in which Paul speaks of the moral depravity of his pagan contemporaries. Alas, what he says very much applies to our own time as well.

The point I am making here is that false worship, including idolatry and, in Roman times, even worship of the emperor himself, corrupts thought. The truth and reality of God is seen in nature. How true this is in our time, when thanks to amazing instruments, we can see faraway galaxies and the tiniest atoms and particles. The stunning reality of nature is such that all humans are "without excuse." The divinity and power of God are clearly seen; to worship creatures is senseless. To do so is to become "futile in [one's] thinking." Those who ignore God will find themselves with "senseless minds," which in time will become "darkened." Such people for a time may think themselves "wise," but in the end they are "fools."

We see the tragic results of such folly all around us. People turn to drugs, legal or otherwise. Political leaders make matters worse by legalizing and decriminalizing the very drugs that harm our minds and bodies. Homeless people stagger about our streets like zombies, their minds often deranged and befuddled with alcohol and drugs. Yet, some of our political leaders wish to make the drugs more readily available and are even distributing syringes and drug paraphernalia. It is madness, and it reflects human thinking that has separated itself from God's thinking.

Others turn to the occult, hoping to find direction and meaning in life. Fortune tellers, palm readers, and necromancers promise to get in touch with the dead and learn something reassuring about life. Really? Instead of turning to God and hearing or reading his Word, there are people who seek the counsel of charlatans.

What today's fools cannot find is peace and the assurance that all is right between them and God. Without God they cannot find the peace of mind that Jesus offers. Long ago the prophet Jeremiah wrote that the man who trusts God "is like a tree planted by water, that sends out its roots by the stream, and does not fear when heat comes, for its leaves remain green, and is not anxious in the year of drought, for it does not cease to bear fruit" (Jeremiah 17:8; cf. Psalm 1:3).

In his masterful way, Jesus gives expression to the same idea when he instructs his followers, "Therefore I tell you, do not be anxious about your life, what you shall eat or what you shall drink, nor about your body, what you shall put on" (Matthew 6:25; cf. 6:31). In a similar verse in Luke, the mind is referenced: "And do not seek what you are to eat and what you are to drink, nor be of anxious mind" (Luke 12:29). The mind that is focused on the Spirit of God is a calm, reassured mind.

Paul warns his readers that to "set the mind on the flesh is death," because "the mind that is set on the flesh is hostile to God; it does not submit to God's law, indeed it cannot" (Romans 8:6, 7). But it doesn't have to be that way. If you "set the mind on the Spirit," you will find "life and peace" (Romans 8:6) and be able to "serve the law of God" (Romans 7:25).

Paul introduces the final section of this magisterial letter to the Romans, in which he lays out the ethics and principles for living, with one of my favorite passages:

> I appeal to you therefore, brethren, by the mercies of God, to present your bodies as a living sacrifice, holy and acceptable to God, which is your spiritual worship. Do not be conformed to this world

but be transformed by the renewal of your mind, that you may prove what is the will of God, what is good and acceptable and perfect.

Romans 12:1–2

Here, Paul brings together both the physical and the mental. He exhorts believers to present themselves to God, body and soul, to his service. To avoid being "conformed to this world," it is necessary to "be transformed by the renewal of your mind." Why? So we "may prove what is the will of God, what is good and acceptable and perfect." Everyone, including Christians, leads very imperfect lives because their minds have not been renewed and they themselves have not been transformed.

I end this chapter by repeating what I said earlier: If you don't take captive your thoughts, they will take you captive. You don't have to do this alone, though. God is with you and will freely make his Spirit available to you. Put your mind on God's Spirit and see the difference it makes.

Why Don't I Feel My Faith?

*An Interview with Psychologist and
Pastor Dr. Ted Witzig Jr.*

Throughout this book we have focused on experiencing God's peace, but what if you don't feel his shalom? How do we navigate feelings of doubt that contradict who we are in Christ Jesus?

As a start to answering these questions, let me ask two more: Have you ever met someone whom you didn't care for initially but learned it was a wrong first impression? Has there been a time or two when you made a bad decision based on incomplete information? I'm guessing your emotions and feelings changed drastically after receiving new, accurate information.

In chapter 24 of the Gospel of Luke, two disciples are walking along the road to Emmaus. They are downcast, even discouraged and upset, because Jesus was crucified. No one expected the Messiah to die by Roman crucifixion. *Perhaps the messianic program is over? Perhaps John the Baptist was wrong?* The two disciples (one is named Cleopas; v. 18) are joined by Jesus himself for a seven-mile walk from Jerusalem to Emmaus, but they don't recognize Jesus. Not realizing they are walking and conversing with the resurrected Messiah, they admit with a particular note of defeat, "We had hoped that he was the one" (Luke 24:21). Then they have a veritable walking Bible study, during which Jesus explains how Moses and the prophets and Scriptures pointed to Jesus himself. The disciples invite the stranger into their home for dinner. Only when Jesus blesses the food do they recognize him and "their eyes [are] opened" (v. 31). They recall, "Did not our hearts burn within us while he talked to us on the road, while he opened to us the scriptures?" (v. 32).

Our feelings are changing all of the time. In the words of the French novelist Gustave Flaubert, "One can be the master of what one does, but never of what one feels." Feelings are not facts. Feelings are not bad, but they can be unreliable and inconsistent. God made us, in his image, with emotions. But our emotions can deceive us. Our feelings do not confirm truth and often contradict God's promises in our lives. Faith is taking God at his word and acting accordingly. Or to put it another way, our relationship with Jesus Christ is not based on feelings but on faith, which is based on the facts of Scripture.

Feelings should never become our truth. They are important, but they are not truth. My friend Dr. William Lane Craig, philosophy professor, says, "When you're going through hard times and God seems distant, apologetics can help you to remember that our faith is not based on emotions, but on the truth, and therefore you must hold on to it."[1]

We have to wrap our feelings in the truth of God's Word, but how? Learning to live by faith and not feelings or emotions (that is, to press forward in faith no matter how we are feeling) is a lifetime journey for everyone, including me, which is why I am delighted to include a tremendous interview with Christian clinical psychologist and pastor Dr. Ted Witzig Jr. (PhD).

"There are certain things we must not pray about—moods, for instance. Moods never go by praying, moods go by kicking. A mood nearly always has its seat in the physical condition, not in the moral. It is a continual effort not to listen to the moods which arise from a physical condition; never submit to them for a second. We have to take ourselves by the scruff of the neck and shake ourselves, and we will find that we can do what we said we could not. The curse with most of us is that we won't. The Christian life is one of incarnate spiritual pluck."—Oswald Chambers

I have had wonderful opportunities to speak in plenary sessions to Christian psychologists, counselors, and therapists from around the world at major conferences with the American Association of Christian Counselors. In my line of work, I have benefited from friendships with many Christian psychologists. You may be surprised how many Christian leaders you know, read, study, and love, also themselves have ongoing sessions with qualified Christian counselors or therapists. Dr. Witzig is one of the finest, clearest, most helpful Christian psychologists I know. It is truly an honor to include his comments in this book on shalom, and I trust it will add great value to our faith and life.

Our Minds Are Tainted by the Fall but Have an Opportunity to Be Renewed

Dr. Witzig, you work and minister at the intersection of psychology and Christian ministry. Give us a brief overview of the human mind and how it functions.

Dr. Witzig: I often explain it this way—God built human beings to function in four areas: biological, psychological, social, and spiritual. While distinct, these areas overlap and can't really be separated. Individually, we are called to be stewards of each of these areas of our lives. In fact, by attending to our personal stewardship of our lives in these areas we are more able to live out the work that God has for us to do and are more able to resist our tendencies to fall prey to our temptations.

I often observe that individuals tend to compartmentalize their lives in unhealthy ways. Instead of viewing their lives as whole beings, they tend to draw heavy distinctions between the four areas. That is, they put an "or" instead of an "and" between those words. When a challenge arises, they ask, "Is this a spiritual thing *or* an emotional thing *or* a relational thing *or* a physical thing?" While some things in life are clearly regarding one facet more than another, living as a Christian involves our whole being.

For example, so much of the Christian story has to do with physical reality, including our bodies. The incarnation required a physical body, and Communion is about bread and wine, things we can touch and taste. As all things are made new in Christ, we will have a new body. The problem is, many Christians make a split, a dualism, between things that are physical and earthly versus spiritual. While they may rightly view the spiritual part as most important, they sometimes view the body or mind as secondary or even unimportant or forgotten altogether.

Sometimes we can identify distinct issues in one of those four areas, but most often each area affects the others; there's a relationship. If you're having trouble sleeping, for example, it can affect you spiritually. (The reality is, it's a lot harder to express the fruit of the Spirit when you're tired!) Conversely, if you're doing well spiritually, you're not always going to have a good night's sleep.

All of us recognize that the liver and heart are organs. If there is a problem with organ function, most of us would not for a minute withhold getting treatment. However, while many Christians (and others) know the brain is also an organ, they often see problems associated with the brain as indicating a problem with their very being. Yes, the brain is a different type of organ than, say, your lungs, but it's an organ nonetheless. If you have diabetes, it's unhealthy to not seek treatment. But when it comes to struggles in our minds, many people hesitate to reach out. Sometimes this is because we may view our mind in the "spiritual category" of our being and then view any problem or struggle as indicating spiritual inferiority. I'm not saying that spirituality doesn't affect our mind; it absolutely does. However, from within the Christian worldview, it is important to recognize that our minds have been tainted by the fall but they can be renewed.

How I Feel Right Now Doesn't Confirm or Deny Truth

Dr. Witzig, we live in a "feelings-driven" culture. Unfortunately, feelings-driven faith has pushed its way into the church. At times, Christians swerve into "the just shall live by feelings, rather than by faith" way of life. Why is this?

Dr. Witzig: I want to answer your question from two perspectives: how human beings process emotions and how secular culture views emotions. First, as human beings, our thoughts come through our minds very much like data. Thought data is not rich in terms of sensory material. But emotions, we embody; we *feel* our emotions. You feel your emotions in your chest and abdomen. You feel the stress in the back of your neck or in the pit of your stomach. Emotions give you real-time feedback about what your body is sensing right then.

Our emotions and sensations are designed to work for us by giving us data about what is going on at the moment. For example, hunger tells you to seek nourishment. Or, if you are out hiking and see a rattlesnake, fear protects you. The problem is that emotions aren't flawless. They're malleable and impacted by a variety of factors. With emotions, we have to be careful we don't vilify or reify them.

Christians (and also unbelievers) accidently fall into an error that says, "This emotion—what I'm feeling—is how I know what is true." The error is a bias whereby we believe we need an emotional confirmation to know something is true. This gets people into serious problems in many ways, but especially in how they view God. The reality is, we all have painful emotions and experiences, and how we feel during those times won't give us the emotional confirmation that the promises of God are true or that God is good.

But Scripture teaches us that God is good even if our circumstances and feelings don't confirm that truth! This is why we must remember what I mentioned previously: the role of emotion is to give us data, to give us information about how we feel at the moment. Importantly, I'm not encouraging anyone to completely disregard their emotions. For example, if you feel uneasy about a relationship or you don't think you can trust a certain person, I'm not telling you to ignore your feelings. We need to always go through a discernment process. If emotions are data, we need to use discernment to seek truth.

Second, as for emotions and culture, secular culture has actually taken this to a whole new level. Secular culture declares, "Emotions and experiences are my truth!" So, if I am in love, then I am going to marry that person, but if I'm out of love, then I am going to leave that person. People sometimes focus more on: "Does this feel right, or does this feel wrong?" Whether it is truth really doesn't matter to them. Our culture has become focused on trying to redefine truth and reality in highly subjective ways. We are observing people in society even going a step further: They say, "How I feel and, especially, when I feel good, this is my identity. If you make me feel bad about or different from that, then you are bad and you are my enemy." It gets very messy. Remember, people have emotions and have experiences. However, truth—as Christ teaches it—is not subjective, based on emotions and experiences.

Faith Is Not What I Feel; Faith Is What I Believe

Dr. Witzig, when properly understood, faith is not a feeling. Rather, faith is active trust based on evidence. Can you elaborate on this?

Dr. Witzig: Faith is what you believe; it's not what you feel. As a psychologist, I love emotions. I love to understand them and talk about them. But remember, your faith is not in your emotions. Your faith is what you believe to be true. We put our faith in Jesus Christ, who is not only worthy of our trust and worthy of our honor, he is a worthy object of our faith.

Sometimes we let emotions cloud biblical truth. I really like Romans 5:1: "Therefore, since we are justified by faith, we have peace with God through our Lord Jesus Christ." Why is this verse so important? A lot of Christians, in practice, fall into the trap of saying, "When I feel at peace, then I will know I am okay with God." But here's the key: Even when I feel emotionally out of sorts, the truth of the Scripture is that because of Christ, God's got me. We all find ourselves on emotional thin ice at times, or experience times when our physical bodies are not well. But that doesn't change the objective truth found in the Word of God.

Faith Equals Trusting God through the Uncertainty

Dr. Witzig, as a Christian psychologist, will you please share steps for believers not to allow their emotions to dictate their faith? For example, many Christians struggle if they doubt their motives, thinking they should feel more love for God than they do sometimes.

Dr. Witzig: I often say that when Scripture and your emotions conflict, first look at the Scripture and bring its truth over your life, and then start walking in the direction of Scripture and let your emotions catch up. Consider the analogy of a train to illustrate this. The train track is the Word of God and the things God has laid out for us. The train engine is our beliefs, values, and commitment to move in the direction of the train track. The caboose is our emotions that come along behind. You don't want to try to operate a train by putting the caboose in front.

When we allow our emotions to dictate our lives, we will either try to make ourselves feel a desired emotion or stop an undesired emotion. We get into trouble when we do that, though. We have very limited ability to make ourselves feel or not feel things. However, cultivating healthy emotions, such as joy and contentment, is the fruit of living in a direction in line with biblical values.

I encourage people to focus on moving in the direction of what they believe is true based on Scripture. I refer to this as "walking faith." Walking faith is about moving in a direction of what you believe is true and the things that you value, even when your emotions aren't fully on board. Walking faith moves you in the direction of God's Word, whether you are feeling it or not.

I love Hebrews chapter 11 and what's known as the "hall of faith"—an account of Old Testaments heroes of the faith. What I find so interesting is that each person mentioned started in a place that was familiar to them. Essentially, they knew where they were and who they were. Then each went through a time of uncertainty, challenge, transition, change, or temptation, but they were deemed righteous. They trusted God through uncertain situations or times. They kept pursuing him. Faith equals trusting God through the uncertainty. Faith is not the absence of feeling uncertain. Faith is moving forward through the uncertainty. Faith is not intolerant of uncertainty.

Don't Let Doubt Become a Toxic Emotion

Dr. Witzig, do you believe doubt is sin? I don't, but when we feel uncertain, does that mean we lack faith?

Dr. Witzig: Oh, wow, that's an awesome question. We use words like *faith*, *doubt*, and *uncertainty* and don't realize how easy it is to merge the different concepts. Here's what I mean: Faith is faith because it's based on belief in what we don't yet see (Hebrews 11:1). The problem is that many times we smuggle in a false assumption: *I have faith when I feel certain.* We accidentally create a false formula in our mind that says "faith = no uncertainty." However, that is not faith. Now, we all love to feel certain. I love to feel certain. It's not wrong to feel certain. But having faith means saying, "Lord, even though I don't understand, I still trust." As believers, we have a lively hope and a confident expectation in God and his promises. It is important for people to not view feeling uncertainty or feeling doubt as the same things as the ongoing refusal to submit to God in unbelief.

We often view doubt in a toxic way. We essentially take doubt—an emotion like any other emotion (anger, sadness, worry, joy, etc.)—and give it the severest of judgments. I don't see faith and doubt as a toxic relationship. Here's what I mean. I believe that Jesus has saved me. He's forgiven me of my sins, and he loves me. Do I understand every facet of that and how it works? No, and that's okay. I don't have to. If I have to be certain about everything in life—meaning, I need comprehensive knowledge of everything, and only then will I feel like I have faith—it's just not that way. Instead of focusing on what I don't understand or focusing on difficult or unsolved questions in my mind, I need to focus on what I do know. I need to focus on what has been revealed. I need to focus on how the Bible says I should be living. And you know what? When I do that, my life is full. Does that mean I'm question-free? No. But the belief that I have to resolve everything to perfect certainty is a Pandora's box. I would much rather people focus on leaning into or walking in the direction of what they believe and know is true, than getting stuck on trying to resolve all doubt.

Too many Christians are racked with shame and doubt, wrongly thinking that because they are a Christian, they should never feel uncertain or anxious about anything. You don't have to know every answer to every question. There's no way to, and, in fact, expecting this of yourself makes doubt feel more toxic. One of the healthiest spiritual practices is to let go of the need to force certainty into the equation. Step back and humbly say, "God, I don't understand this dilemma, and it troubles me. But I will trust you with the mystery, and praise you because you do understand this and everything else that is unclear to me."

Do the Next 5 Percent That You Can

Dr. Witzig, there is much in the Scriptures about trusting God, but so many believers question themselves. They wonder, Am I doing this right? Or, If I really trusted God, I wouldn't feel this way. What is your advice to faithful believers who wonder if they are trusting God enough, and what they should do if they "feel" they are not?

Dr. Witzig: There is a false belief among believers that if they are being faithful, it will always feel like they are on a mountain top. Then, if they struggle to pursue the discipline of prayer or the discipline of being in the Word, they feel like failures. Spiritual disciplines are called *disciplines* for a reason, and sometimes it takes effort in order to read, or pray, or do spiritual things. Ask the most mature Christian you know, "Hey, do you ever struggle to read your Bible?" or "Is it a struggle sometimes to desire to make it to church?" and he or she is going to say, "Of course, I struggle at times." Believing your passion (and emotional feeling) should be 100 percent all the time will leave you discouraged.

I mentioned earlier that *walking faith* is directional. Concern yourself with the direction you are moving. Are you pursuing Jesus Christ? Are you pursuing living in his peace? Are you pursuing living out the teachings of the Sermon on the Mount? Be okay with saying, "While I am not 'there,' and I haven't arrived; I am pursuing it by God's grace!" If you try to pursue the Christian life in an all-or-nothing fashion (I'm either doing it perfectly or I'm failing), you will constantly feel like you are failing.

What we need to do is figure out what the next steps are, and to lean into that space. I tell a lot of people to do the next 5 percent, which might not seem like much. But if you're in New York City and aim toward Los Angeles and then you change the compass settings 5 degrees, you are going to miss Los Angeles by hundreds of miles. The point is, do the next 5 percent that you can. Then focus on doing the next 5 percent. And quit looking at aspects of the Christian life like there's no way you can do them. *I'm in New York, and there's no way that I'm ever going to reach that goal way over there.* Focus on God's grace for today. It is the manna that he provides us each day.

Here is a Scripture that I would recommend: "Draw near to God and he will draw near to you" (James 4:8). It is a simple verse, but when many people feel distant from God, almost the last thing they'll think about doing is to draw near to him and then believe the truth that he will draw near to them. Instead of saying, "I have to feel that verse is true," or "I have to go from feeling distant to perfectly connected," just start walking in the direction of closeness. Start moving toward God and believe that he is going to do his part. He will!

Learning to Live by Faith

Dr. Witzig, learning to live by faith and not by feelings is a lifetime journey. What are the important guardrails and practical steps needed to learn to live by faith and not by our feelings?

Dr. Witzig: First, we need to saturate our minds in truth. Let's make sure we're not trying to follow every new psychological fad before we seek the truth. Our primary pursuit is to follow truth laid out in Scripture: "Sanctify them in the truth; thy word is truth"

"Be not deceived, Wormwood, our cause is never more in jeopardy than when a human, no longer desiring but still intending to do our Enemy's will, looks round upon a universe in which every trace of Him seems to have vanished, and asks why he has been forsaken, and still obeys."—C.S. Lewis, *Screwtape Letters*

(John 17:17). One of the most important things is to identify a group of Scriptures that really speak to you. Memorize them and keep them in front of you. I shared one of mine with you earlier: Romans 5:1.

Second, most of us know many people, but we have few that we are actually deeply connected to, and that is really unfortunate. We were not designed to live the Christian life in isolation. We were designed to thrive in community. Here's what I recommend: Seek to have older, wiser mentors like Paul was in much of the New Testament. They can speak truth into our lives. We also need those who are younger or less mature than us (like Timothy was for Paul) that we are mentoring or bringing up. We also need people in the same stage of life (like a Barnabas) around us for encouragement.

The whole point is that we should not be on our own in this journey. Some of the time I am the one encouraging, admonishing, or challenging others. Some of the time I am one being encouraged, admonished, or challenged. In my counseling work I regularly ask my clients to tell me about their network of support. When I drill down and ask them who in their friend group they actually talk to about their specific struggles, they respond that they don't share with anyone. *Wait, so you are struggling with doubt, or with your purpose, or temptation, or meaning, and no one around you knows about any of it? You weren't meant to go through this alone!* Of course, I think we must choose wisely who we share particular challenges with. I don't think it is helpful to spew our struggles and private issues out on social media, either.

So again, we must first focus on the truth found in the Scriptures. Second, we need community—the Paul, Barnabas, and Timothy model—around us. My third recommendation is to push for more quietness and solitude in minds and souls to meet with God. For me, I have to fight for solitude to listen and "be still." The wonderful thing is that God is always present, but our awareness of his presence is what wanes. When I finally quiet my soul and ask, "What are you saying to me, Lord?" God often points out promises in his Word and for me. And then I need to walk like those teachings are true whether or not my feelings agree.

I am so glad that Hebrews 11:6 says that without faith it is impossible to please God rather than without *feelings of absolute certainty at all times* it is impossible to please God! My faith is in Christ, not in my feelings about faith. Mark 9:24 (NIV)—"I do believe; help me overcome my unbelief!"—is a beautiful passage. People often have read into the Scriptures that believers automatically feel confident when they know the truth and that they never have any corresponding feelings of uncertainty. In Mark 9, Jesus point-blank asks the father, "Do you believe I can do this?" Jesus acted on the Father's faith in him! There is no perfect faith, only faith in a perfect Savior, Jesus Christ! Another beautiful verse is, "When I am afraid, I put my trust in thee" (Psalm 56:3). David took his emotions of fear and turned toward God with them. We struggle because we desire an all-or-nothing faith of a singular emotion of certainty that we want to call faith. However, most of life is in that mixed place of faith in Christ while we have some degree of uncertainty in our emotions, and that is okay! It's really okay. He is faithful.

NOTES

Chapter 1 The Most Important Question of Our Time

1. Ashitha Nagesh, "Strangers Hold onto Man for Two Hours after He Threatens to Jump Off Bridge," *MetroUK*, May 3, 2017, https://metro.co.uk/2017/05/03/strangers-hold-onto-man-for-two-hours-after-he-threatens-to-jump-off-bridge-6612363/.

2. Marina Marcus et al., "Depression: A Global Public Health Concern," *WHO Department of Mental Health and Substance Abuse (2012)*, https://www.who.int/mental_health/management/depression/who_paper_depression_wfmh_2012.pdf.

3. Credit for the phrase "all truth is God's truth" should go to Arthur Holmes (1924–2011), longtime professor of philosophy and English literature at Wheaton College, who wrote a book with that title.

4. "What Is Wellness?" Global Wellness Institute, https://globalwellnessinstitute.org/what-is-wellness/.

5. See C.S. Lewis, "Version Vernacular," *The Christian Century* vol. LXXV (December 31, 1958), 1515, reprinted in *God in the Dock*, pg. 338: "In both countries an essential part of the ordination exam ought to be a passage from some recognized theological work set for translation into vulgar English—just like doing Latin prose. Failure on this paper should mean failure on the whole exam. It is absolutely disgraceful that we expect missionaries to the Bantus to learn Bantu but never ask whether our missionaries to the Americans or English can speak American or English. Any fool can write *learned* language. The vernacular is the real test. If you can't turn your faith into it, then either you don't understand it or you don't believe it."

6. Bob Smietana, "Mental Illness Remains Taboo Topic for Many Pastors," Lifeway Research, September 22, 2014, https://lifewayresearch.com/2014/09/22/mental-illness-remains-taboo-topic-for-many-pastors/.

7. "Nation's Churches Announce Plan to Continue Ignoring Mental Health Issues," *Babylon Bee*, December 27, 2018, https://babylonbee.com/news/nations -churches-announce-plan-to-continue-ignoring-mental-health-issues.

8. Lisa Rudolfsson and Glen Milstein "Clergy and Mental Health Clinician Collaboration in Sweden: Pilot Survey of COPE," *Mental Health, Religion & Culture* (2019), 22(8), 805–818, https://doi.org/10.1080/13674676.2019.1666095.

9. Will Durant, *The Story of Philosophy* (New York: Simon and Schuster, 1961), 20.

10. *American Foundation for Suicide Prevention*, https://supporting.afsp.org /index.cfm?fuseaction=cms.page&id=1226&eventID=5545.

11. "WISQARS Years of Potential Life Lost (YPLL) Report, 1981–2019," *Centers for Disease Control and Prevention*, https://webappa.cdc.gov/sasweb/ncipc /ypll.html.

12. Walter Brueggemann, *Peace* (St. Louis: Chalice Press, 2001), 55.

Chapter 2 Wait, God Wants Me to Be Happy? *Really?*

1. J.M. Twenge et al., "Age, Period, and Cohort Trends in Mood Disorder Indicators and Suicide-Related Outcomes in a Nationally Representative Dataset, 2005–2017," *Journal of Abnormal Psychology* (2019), 128(3), 185–199, https:// doi.org/10.1037/abn0000410.

2. *Shalom* (Hebrew noun), 225 occurrences; *Shalem* (Hebrew verb), 117 occurrences; *Shalem* (Hebrew adjective), 27 occurrences; *Shelem* (Hebrew noun), 87 occurrences; and *Eirene* (Greek noun), 94 occurrences.

3. Timothy Keller, *shalom* article in *NIV Theological Bible*, 2693.

4. G. Hirschfeld, *The Collection of Ancient Greek Inscriptions in the British Museum*, Part IV, 1893, 63–65, inscription no. 894, lines 8–12.

5. Keller, 2694.

Chapter 3 How to Unleash Shalom and Happiness in Your Life

1. J.B. Phillips, *The Price of Success* (Wheaton, IL: Shaw, 1984), 37.

2. Outside of my own readings of J.B. Phillips's books and biographies, I am indebted to a wonderful new website curated by Phillips's grandson, Peter Croft: https://www.jbphillips.org/the-fresh-air-of-heaven.

3. "The Fresh Air of Heaven," Part 3: published, https://www.jbphillips.org /the-fresh-air-of-heaven.

4. For the complete letter from C.S. Lewis to J.B. Phillips, see J.B. Phillips, *The Price of Success*, 100.

5. Phillips, *The Price of Success*, 47.

6. "The Fresh Air of Heaven," Part 4: Opposition and Philosophy, J.B. Phillips Society, https://www.jbphillips.org/the-fresh-air-of-heaven.

7. Phillips, *The Price of Success,* 210.

8. Ibid., 201.

9. Vera Phillips and Edwin Robertson, *J.B. Phillips: The Wounded Healer* (Grand Rapids, MI: Eerdmans, 1984), 110.

10. Ibid., 203.

11. Ibid., 205.

12. Robert J. Morgan, *Worry Less, Live More* (Nashville: W Publishing, 2017), xv.

13. Ibid.

14. Timothy Keller, *The Timothy Keller Sermon Archive* (New York: Redeemer Presbyterian Church, 2013).

15. Research by Robert A. Emmons, reported in "Gratitude Is Good Medicine," *UC Davis Health*, November 25, 2015, https://health.ucdavis.edu/medicalcenter/features/2015-2016/11/20151125_gratitude.html.

16. Gregory Jantz, *The Anxiety Reset* (Downers Grove, IL: Tyndale, 2021), 175.

17. Ralph P. Martin, *Philippians: An Introduction and Commentary*, vol. 11, Tyndale New Testament Commentaries (Downers Grove, IL: InterVarsity Press, 1987), 177.

Chapter 4 The Ministry of Presence

1. Kate Benson, "An Angel Walking among Us at the Gap," *Sydney Morning Herald*, August 1, 2009, https://www.smh.com.au/national/an-angel-walking-among-us-at-the-gap-20090731-e4f2.html.

2. Roger Maynard, "Australia Mourns 'Angel of the Gap' Don Ritchie, the Man Who Talked 160 Out of Suicide," *Independent*, May 16, 2012, https://www.independent.co.uk/news/people/news/australia-mourns-angel-of-the-gap-don-ritchie-the-man-who-talked-160-out-of-suicide-7754339.html.

3. Kathy Marks, "He Invites Suicide Jumpers for a Cup of Tea," *Christian Science Monitor*, October 18, 2010, https://www.csmonitor.com/World/Making-a-difference/2010/1018/He-invites-suicide-jumpers-for-a-cup-of-tea.

4. "Confront Suicidal People, Local Hero Says," *Sydney Morning Herald*, January 25, 2011, https://www.smh.com.au/national/confront-suicidal-people-local-hero-says-20110125-1a42u.html.

5. Marks, "He Invites Suicide Jumpers for a Cup of Tea."

6. Craig S. Keener, *Acts: An Exegetical Commentary: Introduction and 1:1–2:47*, vol. 1 (Grand Rapids, MI: Baker Academic, 2013), 1846. Here I am dependent on Craig Keener's excellent work and personal friendship.

7. Helen Barratt, "RIP Don Ritchie 'the Angel of the Gap' where One Young Woman Survived Her Suicidal Leap but Many More Die," Science 2.0, May 16, 2012, https://www.science20.com/make_love_not_war/blog/rip_don_ritchie_angel_gap_where_one_young_woman_survived_her_suicidal_leap_many_more_die-90124.

8. Jeremiah J. Johnston, *Unanswered: Lasting Truth for Trending Questions* (New Kensington, PA: Whitaker House, 2015), 98.

9. Siang-Yang Tan and Eric Scalise, *Lay Counseling: Equipping Christians for a Helping Ministry* (Grand Rapids, MI: Zondervan, 2016 edition). Please see chapter 4 in their book, especially the second to last paragraph on page 70.

Chapter 5 Jesus Is Our Shalom

1. Robert McCrum, "The 100 Best Novels: No 14—*Vanity Fair* by William Thackeray (1848)," *The Guardian*, December 23, 2013, https://www.theguardian.com/books/2013/dec/23/william-thackeray-vanity-fair-100-best-novels.

2. Caroline Westbrook, "What Is Vanity Fair and What Does It Mean?" *Metro UK*, September 3, 2018, https://metro.co.uk/2018/09/03/what-is-vanity-fair-and-what-does-it-mean-7908803/.

3. John Bunyan, *The Pilgrim's Progress*, vol. 3 (Bellingham, WA: Logos Bible Software, 2006), 127.

4. George R. Beasley-Murray, *John*, vol. 36, Word Biblical Commentary (Dallas: Word, Incorporated, 1999), 378–379.

5. Nicky Gumbel sermon, "Hope for the City: Shalom," Holy Trinity Brompton, September 9, 2018, https://www.htb.org/sunday-talks-archive/2018/9/11/hope-for-the-city-shalom.

6. Luke wrote Luke and Acts (37,932 words), and Paul wrote thirteen books and epistles of the Bible (32,408 words).

7. Leon Morris, *The Gospel According to John* (Grand Rapids, MI: Eerdmans, 1995), 584.

8. Warren Wiersbe, *Be Obedient*, "Be" Commentary Series (Wheaton, IL: Victor Books, 1991), 9.

9. Wiersbe, 110.

10. Charles Ryrie, *Ryrie Study Bible: New American Standard Bible*, expanded ed. (Chicago: Moody Press, 1995), 1442.

11. Mike Gendron sermon, "Are You Sure You're a Christian?" https://compass.org/product/are-you-sure-youre-a-christian-mike-gendron/.

12. I am thankful for the lessons I have personally learned and incorporated in this paragraph from R.B. Thieme Jr.'s work *Christian, at Ease!*

13. Ibid., 15.

14. Ibid., 19.

Chapter 6 Vulnerability Is the New Superpower

1. "The 50 Most Influential Living Philosophers," The Best Schools, March 31, 2021, https://thebestschools.org/features/most-influential-living-philosophers/.

2. The Holy Spirit has strengthened J.P. to the extent that his book *Finding Quiet: My Story of Overcoming Anxiety and the Practices That Brought Peace* is a must for your library.

3. Catherine Soanes and Angus Stevenson, eds., *Concise Oxford English Dictionary* (Oxford: Oxford University Press, 2004).

4. A. Bruk et al., "Beautiful Mess Effect: Self–Other Differences in Evaluation of Showing Vulnerability," *Journal of Personality and Social Psychology* (2018), 115(2), 192–205, https://doi.org/10.1037/pspa0000120.

5. Ralph P. Martin, *2 Corinthians*, vol. 40, 2nd edition, Word Biblical Commentary (Grand Rapids, MI: Zondervan, 2014), 620.

6. *The Holy Bible: English Standard Version* (Wheaton, IL: Crossway Bibles, 2016), 2 Corinthians 12:4.

7. Jeremiah J. Johnston, *Unanswered: Lasting Truth for Trending Questions* (New Kensington, PA: Whitaker House, 2015), 173.

8. Martin, *2 Corinthians*, 618.

9. Ibid., 613.

10. Charles Hodge, *An Exposition of the Second Epistle to the Corinthians* (New York: A. C. Armstrong & Son, 1891), 286–287.

11. Richard Baxter, "Christ Leads me through No Darker Rooms," https://hymnary.org/text/christ_leads_me_through_no_darker_rooms.

12. Martin, *2 Corinthians*, 611.

13. G.G. O'Collins, "Power Made Perfect in Weakness: 2 Cor 12:9–10," *Catholic Biblical Quarterly* 33, no. 4 (1971): 528–537; esp. 531.

14. Ralph P. Martin, *2 Corinthians*, WORD BIBLICAL COMMENTARY, vol. 40 (Grand Rapids, MI: Zondervan, 2014), 615.

15. Peter Ubel et al., "Physicians Recommend Different Treatments for Patients Than They Would Choose for Themselves," *Archives of Internal Medicine*, April 22, 2011, https://jamanetwork.com/journals/jamainternalmedicine/fullarticle/227069.

16. Eric Manheimer, "When Doctors Become Patients," *New York Times*, September 2, 2011, https://www.nytimes.com/2011/09/03/opinion/when-doctors-become-patients.html.

17. Joyce Frieden, "A Doctor's Life at the Nation's Oldest Hospital, Now on TV," MedPage Today, September 25, 2018, https://www.medpagetoday.com/hospitalbasedmedicine/generalhospitalpractice/75311.

Chapter 7 God Is My Shield

1. Leon Morris, *The Gospel According to John*, THE NEW INTERNATIONAL COMMENTARY ON THE NEW TESTAMENT (Grand Rapids, MI: Wm. B. Eerdmans Publishing Co., 1995), 463.

Chapter 8 Therefore, Do Not Be Afraid

1. Yale University Library Catalog, https://hdl.handle.net/10079/bibid/3808173.

2. For an excellent summary of Edwards's life and thought, see William Wainwright, "Jonathan Edwards," *The Stanford Encyclopedia of Philosophy* (Fall 2020 edition), https://plato.stanford.edu/archives/fall2020/entries/edwards/.

3. Jeremy Kimble, "10 Things You Should Know about Jonathan Edwards," Crossway, December 1, 2017, https://www.crossway.org/articles/10-things-you-should-know-about-jonathan-edwards/.

4. C. Mitchell, "Edwards, Jonathan," ed. J.D. Douglas and Philip W. Comfort, *Who's Who in Christian History* (Wheaton, IL: Tyndale House, 1992), 224.

5. I am indebted to the excellent scholarship and friendship of Dr. Michael McMullen, my church history professor at Midwestern Baptist Theological Seminary. Dr. McMullen's book, *The Blessing of God*, was a Gold Medallion finalist in the Inspiration category; see Michael D. McMullen, *The Blessing of God* (Nashville: Broadman & Holman, 2003).

6. Sermon points adapted from Timothy Keller, *Prayer: Experiencing Awe and Intimacy with God* (New York: Penguin, 2016), Kindle Edition. Also, I encourage you to read the complete Edwards's sermon here: "Works of Jonathan Edwards Online," vol. 10 (Yale University Press, 1957–2008), http://edwards.yale.edu/archive?path=aHR0cDovL2Vkd2FyZHMueWFsZS5lZHUvY2dpL

WJpbi9uZXdwaGlsb2sy9nZXRvYmplY3QucGw%2FYy45OjQ6MS53amVv#.Xzg6RS2w7.

7. Ibid.

Chapter 9 The Bible Weaponized and Misread

1. I first learned about this eye-opening statistic through a presentation entitled "Mental Illness and the Human Condition," by Daniel Morehead, MD, Peace of Mind Conference, Tyler, Texas, September 2014. See also Ronald Kessler et al., "Lifetime and 12-Month Prevalence of DSM-III-R Psychiatric Disorders in the United States," *Archives of General Psychiatry* (1994), 51(1):8–19, https://jamanetwork.com/journals/jamapsychiatry/article-abstract/496456.

2. Please see a very helpful YouTube presentation from Dr. Daniel Morehead, "Winning the Battle of Mental Illness," https://www.youtube.com/watch?v=F3e6m2ySynY. Also see Dr. Daniel B. Morehead, *Science over Stigma: Education and Advocacy for Mental Health* (Washington, DC: American Psychiatric Association, 2021). In addition, I recommend Dr. Morehead's interviews and presentations, for example, "Spiritual Resilience and Mental Health," at https://theabbey.us/2020/01/lecture-daniel-morehead-m-d-spiritual-resilience-and-mental-health/ and "Mental Health Data That Will Blow Your Mind," at https://vimeo.com/296536935.

3. See my op-ed for Fox News, https://www.foxnews.com/opinion/why-are-so-many-christians-biblically-illiterate. I also wrote about the modern problem facing many Christians who are "Bible-*ish*" in *Unanswered: Lasting Truth for Trending Questions* (New Kensington: Whitaker House, 2015), 144–148.

4. David Instone-Brewer, "Decoding the Bible: Spiritual Maladies," Premier Christianity, January 21, 2020, https://www.premierchristianity.com/home/decoding-the-bible-spiritual-maladies/1206.article.

5. Ibid.

6. Dr. Stanford's paper can be found here: http://www.baylorisr.org/wp-content/uploads/stanford_perceptions.pdf. Also, Dr. Stanford has produced tremendous materials related to the role of the church in helping mental illness.

7. Dr. Morehead's lecture notes are found at https://authorzilla.com/6JLDE/dr-morehead-39-s-notes-mental-illness-and-the-human-nami-austin.html.

Chapter 10 Holistic Happiness: Mind, Body, and Soul

1. I encourage you to find out more information about disease prevention and optimum health by learning more about Dr. Rick Tague and the Center for Nutrition and Preventive Medicine at https://taguenutrition.com.

2. The information presented in this book is not intended to replace a one-on-one relationship with a qualified health care professional and is not intended as medical advice.

Chapter 11 Let's Save Lives

1. Please consider utilizing the *Unanswered: Lasting Truth for Trending Questions* book and Bible study; see Jeremiah J. Johnston, *Unanswered: Lasting Truth*

for Trending Questions Six-Week Bible Study (Nashville: Lifeway, 2015, reprinted 2019); Jeremiah J. Johnston, *Unanswered: Lasting Truth for Trending Questions* (New Kensington, PA: Whitaker House, 2015).

2. I encourage you to read my article with the same title at *RELEVANT* magazine: https://relevantmagazine.com/god/church-invisible-diseases/.

3. See https://www.who.int/news-room/fact-sheets/detail/suicide.

4. Sarah Eekhoff Zylstra, "1 in 4 Pastors Have Struggled with Mental Illness, Finds Lifeway and Focus on the Family," September 22, 2014, https://www.christianitytoday.com/news/2014/september/1-in-4-pastors-have-mental-illness-lifeway-focus-on-family.html.

5. Johnston, *Unanswered* (Bible Study).

6. Ibid.

7. These questions are adapted from the San Francisco Suicide Prevention *Myths and Facts* webpage: http://www.sfsuicide.org/prevention-strategies/myths-and-facts/.

8. Frank Minirth and Paul Meier, *Happiness Is a Choice* (Grand Rapids, MI: Baker Books, 2013), 33.

9. Ibid.

10. I am thankful for email correspondence and sermon notes provided to me from Pastor Harold Warner and his excellent sermon "A Light in the Darkness."

11. Daniel Morehead, "Mental Illness and the Human Condition" presentation, Peace of Mind Conference (Tyler, TX: September 14, 2015).

12. Stephen Altrogge. "Is Mental Illness Actually Biblical?" *Bible Study Tools.* Available at: http://www.biblestudytools.com/blogs/stephen-altrogge/is-mental-illness-actually-biblical.html.

Chapter 12 The Unpardonable Sin

1. Peter La Baume et al., *Wissenschaftliche Kataloge des Römisch-Germanischen Museum* (Cologne, Germany: 1975), 496.

2. Franz Buecheler, ed., *Carmina Latina Epigraphica* (Leipzig, Germany: 1895, 1926), 801.

3. *Corpus Inscriptionum Latinarum* (Berlin, 1862–), 2.1088.

4. Ibid., 8.8567.

5. La Baume, 8.8567.

6. Ibid., 497.

Chapter 13 Mind Wars

1. The translation is found in M.O. Wise et al., *The Dead Sea Scrolls: A New Translation* (San Francisco: HarperCollins, 1996).

2. Josh Howerton tweet, January 22, 2020: https://twitter.com/howertonjosh/status/1219980864702107648.

3. Rick Warren, quoted in Saddleback Church tweet, March 24, 2019: https://twitter.com/Saddleback/status/1109893594129883136.

4. Charles Stanley, *When the Enemy Strikes* (Nashville: Thomas Nelson, 2004), 73.

5. Adam Grant tweet, January 29, 2020: https://twitter.com/AdamMGrant /status/1222537799288655873.

Chapter 14 Why Don't I Feel My Faith?

1. William Lane Craig, *On Guard: Defending Your Faith with Reason and Precision* (Colorado Springs: David C. Cook, 2010), 21.

ABOUT THE AUTHOR

Jeremiah J. Johnston, PhD, MA, MDiv, BA, is a New Testament scholar, author, Bible teacher, and apologist, and he ministers internationally as president of Christian Thinkers Society. Jeremiah's passion is working with local churches and pastors in equipping Christians to give intellectually informed reasons for what they believe. Driven by the Great Commandment, Jeremiah's calling and the mission of Christan Thinkers Society is to equip Christians to love God with all their hearts and minds.

Jeremiah has distinguished himself speaking in churches of all denominations, and authored articles in both popular magazines and scholarly books, journals, and media programs. As a theologian, who has the unique ability to connect with people of all ages, and as a culture expert, he has been interviewed numerous times and contributed articles across a spectrum of national shows, including: *Fox News, CNN, CBS This Morning, Vanity Fair, Premier Christianity* magazine and *Premier* radio, *RELEVANT* magazine, *DECISION* magazine, the *Christian Post*, the Moody Radio Network, and the Salem Radio Network.

As a New Testament scholar, Johnston has published with Oxford University Press, E. J. Brill, Bloomsbury T & T Clark, Macmillan, and Mohr Siebeck. He completed his doctoral residency in

Oxford in collaboration with Oxford Centre for Missions Studies and received his PhD from Middlesex University (UK). He has also earned advanced degrees in theology from Acadia University and Midwestern Baptist Theological Seminary. Jeremiah is married to Audrey, and they are parents to five children—Lily Faith, Justin, and the triplets: Abel, Ryder, and Jaxson!

facebook.com/ChristianThinkersSociety
twitter.com/ jeremiahj
instragram.com/ jeremiahj
ChristianThinkers.com

More from
Jeremiah J. Johnston

In a day when Christians are often attacked for their beliefs, this provocative and enlightening book looks at the positive influence of Christianity, both historically and today. *Unimaginable* guides readers through the halls of history to see how Jesus' teachings dramatically changed the world and continue to be the most powerful force for good today.

Unimaginable

CPSIA information can be obtained
at www.ICGtesting.com
Printed in the USA
LVHW030924201122
733280LV00042B/2654